Classic
COUNTRY TOYS

Classic
COUNTRY TOYS

BRUCE WEXLER

Skyhorse Publishing

Skyhorse Publishing books may be purchased in bulk at special discounts for sales promotion, corporate gifts, fund raising, or educational purposes. Special editions can also be created to specifications. For details, contact the Special Sales Department, Skyhorse Publishing, 555 Eighth Avenue, Suite 903, New York, NY 10018 or info@skyhorsepublishing.com.

www.skyhorsepublishing.com

ACKNOWLEDGMENTS:
Tom and Wendy Beck—The World's Largest Toy Museum, Branson, Missouri.
J. P. Bell—Photography
David Wallace—Bus Collection
Designed by **Sue Rose**

10 9 8 7 6 543 2 1
Library of Congress Cataloging-in-Publication Data

Wexler, Bruce, 1962-
 Classic country toys / Bruce Wexler.
   p. cm.
 ISBN 978-1-60239-758-3 (alk. paper)
1. Toys—Collectors and collecting—United States. I. Title.
 NK9509.65.U6W48 2009
 688.7'20973—dc22
                              2009017310
 ISBN 978-1-60239-758-3

Printed in China

CONTENTS

INTRODUCTION

Toys are designed to be both entertaining and educational. A child's imagination of what it will be like to grow up in the real world is shaped by toys. To own a toy car or to play with a doll or stuffed dog can lead to one day owning the real thing. Many toys present exciting and dangerous aspects of the real world in a safe, play environment—i.e., toys like railroad trains, steam rollers, trucks, cars, fire engines, toy guns, stoves, and even electric irons.

Toys are a wonderful barometer of historical change and popular culture. From the charming cast iron "Hillclimbers" and piggy banks made in Ohio at the turn of the 19th century to the sheet metal toys made in Detroit and Moline from scrap steel in the early days of the automobile industry to the rubber toys of failing tire manufacturer Auburn to the printed tin Marx "nickel and dime" toys from the years of the Great Depression to the wooden toys made during the material-starved 1940s to the cowboy guns and western gear of the affluent 1950s, and movie- and TV-influenced character toys of the 1960s and 70s, every toy reflects the times and tastes of the era it originates from.

We have carefully selected toys that have particular associations with the traditional countryside and landscape of America. Toys based on country characters like Howdy Doody, Woody, and the *Dukes of Hazzard*; trucks, buses, and cars that traverse the great highways and country roads; tractors that plow the fields; a travelling circus bringing entertainment to the small towns; and farm trucks that haul the produce to the big cities—you'll find all these illuminated in the following pages.

THE FERRYGO TWIN

The Ferrygo Twin is a pull-along toy riverboat with twin paddle wheels and four small rollers underneath that allow it to glide over the floor. What remains of the original pull-string fixing can be seen on the prow. The toy is a charming piece made in the late 1920s of pressed tin assembled with lugs.

It has colorful lithographed detailing in the style of manufacturers such as Wolverine, although there are no visible brand markings.

The beam on the upper deck rocks when the toy is pulled along.

The intricate graphics include a group of passengers, opulent arched windows, and the patent date, September 27, 1927.

8

BICO BUS

Route 29 to Joyville is the destination of this colorful open-topper made in Germany circa 1920 and marketed in the U.S. as a Bico toy. It is made from tinplate with printed graphics. A selling point of this toy is the conductor who fits in a slot in the upper deck and moves up and down. Sadly, he is missing from this well-played-with example, but a few of the tinplate passengers still survive. The wheels are set on a left-hand lock, making the bus move around in circles. It is eight and a half inches long.

The clockwork motor is mounted here and has a fixed key.

9

MARX BUS TERMINAL

The roadway outside the terminal has three Tootsietoy buses waiting to depart.

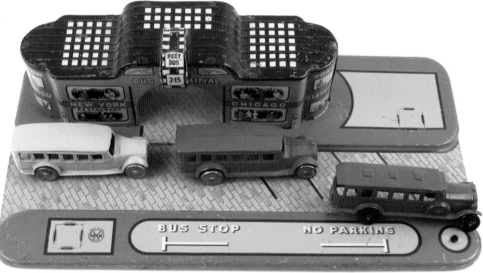

This toy is evocative of the days when bus terminals across the land gave country people access to the big cities. Marx made this charming tinplate bus station in the 1930s.

Its detailed graphics include the Greyhound logo, phone booths, a restaurant, a clock, and destinations such as Cleveland, Chicago, New York, and St. Louis. It is twelve inches long.

TURNER BUS

This is a large, sturdy toy. The long hood is typical of this era.

Despite a few surface dents, the pressed-steel auto has withstood ninety years of play.

This Overland Bus is a wonderful example of a large, pressed-steel toy bus of the 1920s. John C. Turner of Dayton, Ohio manufactured it. This realistic toy, twenty-six inches long, would probably have seemed very much like the "real thing" to a young bus operator. The Turner Company made a number of toy vehicles in this style, and their 1931 catalog promises that their toys are "made of heavy auto steel, substantially constructed, beautifully finished in gay, flashy, colored enamels which are baked on." What more could a discerning child want?

AMISH BUGGY AND BELL TOY

This Amish buggy was made in the 1890s. A. C. Williams of Ravenna, Ohio constructed it from cast iron. The detailing on the casting is exceptional, with items such as the driver, steps, lamps, and horse's tack clearly distinguishable. It is five inches long.

Cast-iron toys were popular in the latter half of the nineteenth century.

There are still faint traces of the toy's original bright blue, red, and brown enamel.

The Bell Toy is a cast-iron horse drawing a chiming gong on wheels; it makes a chiming sound as it is pulled along. The Gong Bell Manufacturing Company of East Hampton, Connecticut made it in the 1870s.

12

AUBURN RUBBER MOTORCYCLES

Many toy manufacturers started by making products aimed at adults. The Double Fabric Tire Company was founded in 1913 in Auburn, Indiana. Its business was to manufacture tires for the town's eponymous auto company. But as Auburn's production fell away, the company looked to diversify into other rubber products. By 1935, these included toys. Here are three examples of Auburn Rubber toys from the late 1930s. They are: a standing traffic cop in light blue and five-inch and nine-inch mounted police officers.

The rubber castings are surprisingly detailed. The large police officer's face and uniform and the bike's spoked wheels, engine, and gearbox are all clearly defined.

The colors, which are made by adding dye to the latex solution, have stood the test of time.

13

CAST-IRON CARS

In the early years of toy cars, cast iron was the most popular material. Henry H. Dent of Fullerton, Pennsylvania started the Dent Hardware Company in 1898. The company produced miniature horse-drawn farm wagons, carriages, and trains. The Yellow Cab dates from the 1920s. It is seven and a half inches long and the body is cast in two halves.

The black Ford was made by Arcade. Arcade was another cast-iron novelty company and was located in Freeport, Illinois. The car dates from 1923 and doubles as a money bank; dual-purpose novelties were a company speciality. Arcade also made a famous version of the Yellow Cab.

This cast iron car from 1923 doubles as a money bank.

The Yellow Cab shows the finer points of Dent's detailed castings.

DAYTON COUPE

Skilled immigrants from the European toy manufacturing centers immigrated to Ohio in the nineteenth century. This led to the establishment of a thriving toy industry there, and Dayton in particular became a hub where many toys were made. This coupe from the 1920s shows how pressed-steel toys had improved by this time. It has excellent detailing such as the clearly-defined radiator grill, door panels, hood louvers, beaded edge, running boards, and spoked wheels. The blue enamel paint is original.

This toy reflects car styling of the 1920s. It may be based on the Studebaker Light Six.

DAYTON FRICTION AUTOS

The development of the patented Boyer friction mechanism in Dayton, Ohio led to the town becoming a center of toy manufacture. Dayton's preeminence began in the final years of the nineteenth century and lasted well into the twentieth century. Boyer friction was a breakthrough in powered toys: pressing the toy along the floor and then releasing it charged the mechanism. The cars shown here

An interesting feature of this toy is the small, cast-iron figure of the lady driver. She is dressed in formal motoring clothes.

are copies of current cars of the early 1900s. They are quite crudely made, constructed with flat sections of steel that were then bent to shape. Cast-iron wheels were then attached with single rod spindles. Although simple, the steel construction of these toys has enabled them to withstand the test of time.

16

DISTLER SEDAN

Many toys found their way into toy stores across America from long-established toy makers in Europe. Johan Distler of Nuremberg—a picturesque Bavarian city that was a center of the German toy industry in the early twentieth century—manufactured this fine four-door sedan that dates from the 1920s. It is made from pressed steel, but also has advanced features such as a clockwork motor, battery-operated headlights, and an illuminated rear license plate.

Note the entry for the clockwork key above the left-hand running board. The car has detailed graphics on its wheels and tires.

17

FORD BRONCO

Toy cars always reflect trends in the real "grown-up" motor industry. Ford launched the Bronco in 1966. It was a small but rugged SUV that brought modern styling to the off-road market—Ford's answer to the Willys Jeep. Little guys everywhere wanted to own a toy version. The Nylint Company of Rockford, Illinois licensed this version. Nylint produced pressed-steel toys from 1945 onward. In fact, the company specialized in Ford vehicles between 1959 and 1974. They used highly recognizable Ford detailing such as grill badges and embossed tailgates. During these years, Nylint also made models of the company's new cars as promotional giveaways for Ford dealerships. The Bronco model was one of Nylint's signature toys.

This blue Ford Bronco is a real boy's toy!

GUMBY'S JEEP

Starting as a humble pile of modeling clay in 1953, Gumby went on to have his own television show. His inventor, Art Clokey, introduced him on *The Howdy Doody Show* in 1956. He had a regular spot on the show until he got his own program, *The Gumby Show*. During the 1960s, his popularity continued to grow and Lakeside Toys of Minneapolis, Minnesota produced a range of Gumby merchandise. Serious collectors would tell you that these two bendy action figures of Gumby and Pokey (Gumby's loyal horse), which can be posed with "Gumby's Jeep," are totally collectible. Lakeside even produced costumes for the figures to wear. The bright yellow Jeep has chrome bumpers, a steering wheel, a fold-down windshield, and "mud-grip" tires.

While Gumby appears relaxed, Pokey looks a little stressed, with his legs sticking through the windshield!

The smiling face of a character that has amused millions.

19

HILLCLIMBER AUTO

The toy shows more than a trace of its former glory: a bright red and gold enamel finish.

"Hillclimber" is a trademark for toys that can climb a slope using a patented mechanism. This works with a weighted flywheel that can store energy from a "push" to propel the toy auto uphill. The device was invented by Israel Donald Boyer and was patented as the "Locomotive Toy Mechanism."

Manufacture of these toys was centered around Dayton, Ohio in the late nineteenth century, where Schiebel Toys held the copyright to the mechanism. In 1909, the company took legal action against rival manufacturer D. P. Clarke of the Dayton Friction Works; Clarke had marketed his products as "Hillclimbers," believing the term to be the generic name for this type of toy. This particular Hillclimber is a very early automobile. It has two cast figures—a lady and a little girl—dressed in nineteenth-century apparel.

JEEPS

Jeeps have always been popular toys; they are open-topped and can be used with action figures. Marx made the top jeep from pressed steel. It dates from the early 1950s, its age betrayed by the lithographed, pressed metal wheels and tires. Later models, like the Tonka (below), had plastic wheels and tires. But the Marx, with its red and yellow interior and fold-down hood, is still a nice-looking toy with battery-operated headlights. The guy leaning on the windshield is an eight-inch-tall Tonka Action Figure. He is made of hard plastic and his blue (non-removable) Stetson has the word "Tonka" molded into it. The lower Jeep is also by Tonka, who became serious rivals to Marx during the 1960s by offering more details in their toys, including pierced grills, opening bonnets, and realistic wheels (complete with cool chrome hubcaps and tires with treads).

The Tonka action figure is wearing sunglasses. His arms, legs, and head all move.

21

MARX AMBULANCE

This rare, surviving Marx tinplate ambulance dates from the 1930s. During World War II, Marx also made a military version in olive green paint. It is a wind-up toy and has a very loud siren—a combination that made the ambulance totally irresistible to young boys. The fixed key for the motor is at the bottom of the right-hand door. It has period features including the original red and cream paint, fully lithographed graphics, running boards, rubber tires, and an opening back door. The toy is of a pleasing scale (it is a full fourteen inches long) and has a weighty feel that later plastic toys never had.

The handsome Marx paint job has stood the test of time very well.

MARX COUPE

By the early 1930s, toy maker Louis Marx was rising to become known as the Henry Ford of the toy industry. By offering exceptional value per dollar, Marx toys were able to survive the depression.

The coupe shown here dates from that period and was offered at a very competitive price. It also appeared in several other guises in the Marx range, so development costs were already covered for subsequent versions. It was a tinplate, wind-up toy with battery-operated headlights. The body was adorned in a two-tone cream and red paint scheme with printed-on detailing, including the hood louvers and doors.

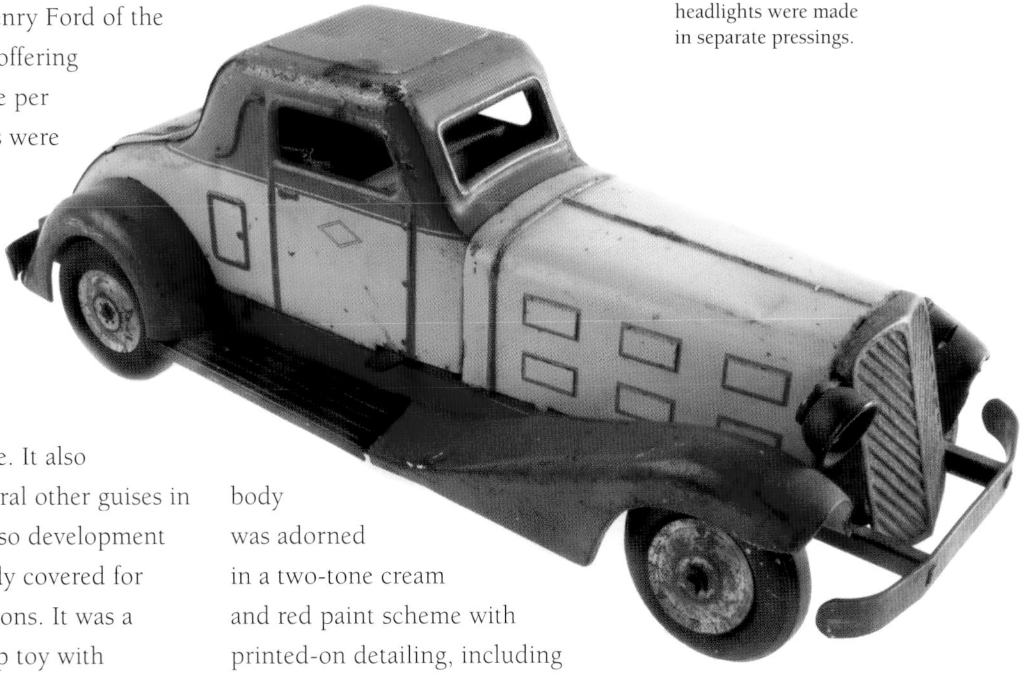

Realistic details like the grill, running boards, bumpers, and headlights were made in separate pressings.

23

MOTORCYCLE COP

If ever there was a toy that could be described as "pure Americana," this is it. The Champion Hardware Company of Geneva, Ohio was in business from 1883 to 1954, making novelty household products in cast iron. But during the depression of the 1930s, sales of household goods plummeted and Champion turned to toys. Its range included Chrysler Airflow, Plymouth, and REO coupes. They also made trucks like the Gas & Motor Oil Truck. However, the company's signature toy was this cast-iron motorcycle cop, finished in blue enamel with flesh

The toy is delightfully detailed and has "Champion" proudly embossed on the gas tank.

tones to the face and hands. It also had red wheel hubs and white rubber tires. This is the CM3 model. The model came in different sizes; this one is seven and three quarter inches long.

PICKUPS

Here are toys by two of America's leading metal toy manufacturers, head to head: a green Buddy L and a red Tonka. Both are models of 1950s Ford pickups. Buddy L toy production started in 1921 when Fred Lundahl, the founder of the Moline pressed-steel Company, took some samples of a toy he had made for his son Arthur (or "Buddy") to the New York Toy Fair. By 1925, Lundahl had a range of twenty toys. The unique selling point was that the toys were made from the same materials as real cars; Lundahl initially used scrap steel from his manufacturing business. His toys were also very realistic, and their design closely followed that of the real thing. Like Buddy L, Tonka's original core business was not toys; in Tonka's case, it was garden tools. The company switched over to toys when that market proved much stronger.

Both trucks are in good shape despite fifty years of play.

PICKUP AND TRAILER

Nylint Toys were renowned for their accuracy, as shown by these detailed tires and chrome-plated wheel hubs.

Children love toy trucks that tow trailers; the thrill of transporting stuff in the back is perennial. This Tonka pickup from the early 1960s is paired with a Nylint farm trailer. Tonka, a Minnesota company, is named for the Sioux word meaning "great," which aptly describes the toys. They are solidly constructed and designed to be handed down.

The livery of this steel step side pickup is the standard Tonka red of the period. The grill and headlight assembly is tarnished but still intact, but the hubcaps have been removed. The model is twelve and a half inches long. The Nylint green horse cart is from the company's popular farm set.

The cleverly designed Tonka one-piece plastic wheel molding uses bracing struts for extra strength.

26

RACING CAR

This is an early cast-iron toy that celebrates the dawn of performance motoring. This elegant boat-tail speedster has the appearance of an early toy by the A.C. Williams Company of Ravenna, Ohio. It predates the retirement of company founder, Adam Clark Williams; small, cast-iron toys like this one were Williams's specialty. The company was particularly known for money banks, racecars, and aircraft. The car has spoked, cast-iron wheels (which were originally enameled or nickel-plated) and peened axles. The car has some body detailing in the casting including hood ports, a radiator cap, and door fittings. The driver was cast in one piece with the car, but some models had separate drivers. The car is eight inches long.

The cast iron is back to its natural state here with very few traces of paint remaining.

RED COUPE

This magnificent large toy is eighteen and a quarter inches long. Made from pressed steel, the car has no markings but is strongly redolent of the Ohio toy industry; it may be an American National product from Toledo, Ohio. It probably dates from the late 1920s, when the company was a competitor of Keystone and Buddy L. The coupe has a long hood, an impressive radiator, and running boards. It has pressed-steel, ventilated wheels and a spare on the rumble seat lid. The red paint appears to have been retouched at some time.

A toy of this size invariably encourages a child to ride on it, and the coupe lid has suffered as a result.

28

SCARAB

Buddy L built this charming, two-seater roadster circa 1936. It is named for the Egyptian dung beetle that gave design inspiration to a whole series of contemporary cars. Like all Buddy L toys, its pressed-steel construction was robust, long-lasting, and mechanically advanced. The scarab features a cam-operated steering mechanism activated by a spur gear linked to the rear axle. The car is powered by a clockwork motor, and has a crew of two intricately lithographed, 1920s-style occupants. It also has body details including a windshield, a grill, and winged side embellishments. It is ten and a half inches long.

The overall impression of this scarab is of a wonderfully patinated toy in good condition. It has survived over seventy years of use.

STAGECOACH

This stagecoach is a beautifully-detailed, cast-iron toy. It has great lines that exude a sense of speed and flowing movement.

stagecoach dates from the late 1930s, when western toys were still popular. The coach body is cast in two halves and held together with a screw and nut fixing, which can be seen on the side of the door. The cast-iron wheels rotate on steel spindles and the body framing is picked out in gold paint. The two cantering horses are mounted on either side of the shaft. There is a trailing wheel underneath the coach that allows it to be pulled along. The driver is resplendent in full "forty-niner" garb. The stagecoach is eleven inches long.

Cast-iron toys persisted into the 1930s but then suffered due to the war effort. At this time, many toys were handed in to be melted down to make arms, tanks, aero engines, and other military equipment. This has greatly increased the desirability of surviving examples of cast-iron toys from companies like Kenton and Arcade. This fine

TN POLICE JEEP

This neat police vehicle is a tin toy dating from the 1960s. It was made by Nomura of Japan and marketed under the "TN" brand name. The two cops have lithographed uniforms that detail their collars and ties, badges, pockets, and brown leather gauntlets. They also have swiveling arms. The passenger's Stetson is not original, even though it looks the part. The jeep is battery-powered and has working headlights and red flashing lights on the front fenders. It has great detail including rubber tires, a fire extinguisher, grab handles on the hood, wheel trims, yellow seats, a parking brake, and a police radio.

These guys look as though they mean business!

TONKA PICKUPS

The black pickup shows signs of lots of play. Tailgates always seem to go missing!

a reputation for durability and realism. Pickups were added to the range in 1955 and were popular because kids could load other toys into the back. Mound made sure that their vehicle range didn't become stale and they kept it in line with development of real-life models. The vehicle on the far right is a truck from 1958 based on the Ford F-100. It advertises "Gambles, The Friendly Store" from nearby St. Louis Park, Minnesota. Next to that

Just after World War II, six cash-strapped Minnesota teachers set up the Mound Metalcraft Company. They began by making hand tools for gardeners in the basement of the local schoolhouse, but in 1947, they acquired a toy company owned by Edward C. Streater and went into steel toy production. Their toys soon gained

Tonka added graphics and stick-on plastic decals. These were popular in the 1980s.

is an AA Wrecker Truck offering twenty-four hour service. This was based on the 1961 Ford F-100. On the adjacent page are examples of the company's 1980s range, which includes two Chevy-based trucks with more zingy decals.

Left: The wheels are nicely detailed and have the words "Tonka Toy" embossed on the tire wall.

Right: The condition of this pickup would count against it in the value stakes, but it is still an interesting piece.

TOOTSIETOY

Samuel Dowst of the Dowst Manufacturing Company of Chicago invented this die-cast toy. Dowst watched his linotype machine producing cast-metal type and was struck by the idea that the machine could also cast other objects. He produced the first die-cast metal toy cars, using the same lead alloy as was used to produce type. He produced his first successful model, a miniature Model T Ford, in 1906. In 1922, Dowst was looking for a brand name for his toys and decided to use the name of his brother's granddaughter, Tootsie. Nathan Shure bought the company in 1926, and in 1934, switched to using a new zinc-based alloy,

The toy was more successful than the car, selling by the millions.

Mazac. The toy featured here is a Graham Blue Streak Eight from 1932. Designed by Amos Northup, and with body detailing by Raymond Dietrich, it was a pretty cool car in its day—the first to use full-skirted fenders, a trend soon generally adopted by the auto industry.

TURNER PACKARD

The Packard was powered by a friction motor and has advanced features such as battery-powered headlights.

John C. Turner started as a worker at the D. P. Clarke Company of Dayton, Ohio. It is believed that Clarke used Turner's innovative ideas to improve his toys, so it is unsurprising that Turner decided to use his skills to make his own fortune. In the 1920s, Turner set up his own company in nearby Wapakoneta, Ohio. This splendid model is based on the Packard 1922 Single Six Roadster. It is twenty-six inches long.

35

U.S. MAIL MOTORCYCLE

This classic toy dates from the 1930s and was made by the Hubley Manufacturing Company of Lancaster, Pennsylvania. John E. Hubley founded the company in 1894. In its early years, it specialized in cast-iron toys like this one, but Hubley later moved on to die-cast alloy. The company promoted its toys with the slogan "they're different"—meant to refer to Hubley's great attention to detail.

This motorcycle has moving handlebars with rubber grips, a lifelike engine casting, footrests, and spoked wheels complete with rubber tires. The toy was cast in three parts and assembled with screws.

Even after eighty years, the Indian logo is clearly visible on the gas tank.

WYANDOTTE LASALLE

The pressed metal wheels, complete with rubber tires, run on axles that are housed in the fenders.

This magnificent toy was made by Wyandotte, a company that grew up in the heart of "Motor City." Wyandotte used its location to its advantage and benefited from skilled workers and cheaper materials (such as recycled steel). The company carefully followed modern auto model design and as a result, their toys followed closely on the heels of the real thing. Perhaps Wyandotte was able to peek at the sketchbooks of the automakers' design studios? This red, pressed-steel LaSalle is an exaggerated depiction of the 1937 sedan. It has a more outrageously raked windshield, bulging fenders, and the longest hood imaginable. The toy is powered by an inertia motor, which is activated by pulling the car backwards and then letting it go. It is thirteen and three eighths inches long.

37

WYANDOTTE COUPE

The coupe's retractable roof is still in full working order.

Wyandotte was situated in close proximity to the hub of American car production in Michigan, just a stone's throw from the major plants. In the austere times of the 1940s, it is likely that the full-size car manufacturers encouraged toy companies to make miniature versions of their models to promote their latest designs. This pressed-steel toy is strongly reminiscent of Pontiac's styling in the late 1940s. The silver side streak detail recalls Frank Hershey's torpedo styling, and the woody effect was also very popular at that time.

BARBIE

Ruth Handler, co-founder of Mattel, took inspiration from her daughter Barbara, who made paper dolls and imagined them in the "grown-up" world. Ruth devised a unique concept for a teenage fashion model doll and Barbie debuted at the 1959 New York Toy Fair. The first Barbie was dressed in a black and white striped swimsuit with a signature ponytail. She stood eleven and a half inches tall and retailed for $3.00, though these original dolls are worth thousands of dollars today. Through the years, Barbie has reflected her keen interest in fashion, while remaining feminine and demure. Several famous designers have created outfits for her, including Yves St. Laurent, Christian Dior, Versace, and John Paul Gaultier. Fashion icons such as Jackie Kennedy and Madonna have also inspired Barbie's clothes.

Right: 1960s Barbie steps out in a trendy checked blouse and jeans.

Above left: Barbie became a princess in the 2000s.

39

BLACK DOLL

This historic folk-art doll is based on a black "Mammy" character and is part of a long tradition of black American dolls dating back to pre-Civil War days. Many of the early dolls were often homemade from various scraps of cloth but this is a later, factory-made china doll. Several manufacturers, including Reliable, made dolls of this kind from rubber in the 1940s and 50s. The 1960s was a fertile time for black dolls, with additions to popular ranges of doll such as Thumbelina, a Babyland rag doll, Ideal's Black Velvet doll, and finally a black Barbie.

Mammy dusts her toy stove made by Keystone.

BONNIE BRAIDS

Bonnie Braids is the daughter of comic strip character Dick Tracy and his wife, Tess Truehart. This doll's birth date was May 4, 1951. According to legend, she was born on the backseat of a taxicab on the way to the hospital. Toy company Ideal manufactured her with a vinyl head and a hard plastic body. She has jointed arms but her signature feature is her special molded hair with two yellow braids attached to the sides of her head. She was on sale for just two years, from 1951 to 1953, so surviving examples are naturally harder to find than dolls with longer production runs.

Bonnie Braids comes with her own wardrobe (literally).

41

CABBAGE PATCH DOLL

In 1982, in their first year of mass-market production, no less than three million Cabbage Patch Kids were sold.

As an art student in 1976, Xavier Roberts adapted an early 19th-century German technique of fabric sculpture and combined it with his mother's quilting skills to create the "soft sculpt" effect so distinctive to the Cabbage Patch Dolls. Roberts was still a teenager when he started the Babyland General Hospital in Cleveland, Georgia where customers came to "adopt" a doll that came with full adoption papers. Roberts then started the Original Appalachian Artworks company to produce the dolls. The Coleco toy company was excited about Roberts's original ideas and began to mass-market the dolls under their new brand name, the Cabbage Patch Kids.

DUKES OF HAZZARD

What could be more country than these *Dukes of Hazzard* goodies? The cult-status CBS TV show aired from 1979 to 1985. It revolved around the antics of the Duke family and their struggles with Boss Hogg, the corrupt Commissioner of Hazzard County. The eight-inch action figure of Bo Duke is by Mego. But for many viewers, the real star of the show (apart from Daisy Duke) was the Dukes' amazing car, the "General Lee." Shown here is the famous Ertl 1:18 scale model of the distinctive, bright red Dodge Charger. The real car was involved in numerous outrageous car chases, where it never failed to outrun the police car of Boss's incompetent accomplice, Sheriff Rosco P. Coltrane.

The show's affiliations were quite clear with the Confederate flag on General Lee's roof and its horn playing the first few bars of Dixie!

43

HOWDY DOODY

In 1947, the *Howdy Doody Show*, featuring a marionette named Howdy Doody and his human companion, Buffalo Bob Smith, aired on IBC. The characters were residents of Doodyville, an imaginary Western town, and the entertainment was a combination of slapstick comedy and amusing observations about life in the West.

The show ran for over 1,000 episodes until 1960. Howdy had blue eyes and freckles painted onto his composition head, red molded hair, and a mouth that moved up and down to simulate speech. His Western-style clothing consisted of blue jeans, plaid shirt, red bandana, and cowboy boots. The show used three versions of Howdy: the main

puppet: a duplicate for prolonged camera shots named Double Doody: and a doll without strings used for still photography called Photo Doody. Rufus Rose, the puppeteer, donated one of the original puppets to the Smithsonian in 1980.

Naturally, children wanted puppets to play with. Our example is one of the commercially available toys from the 1950s, which is sixteen inches tall.

A close-up of Doody's mouth showing the hinged lower lip, which enabled him to give voice to his pearls of wisdom.

KEWPIE DOLL

The Kewpie doll was based on Rose O'Neill's illustrations of cherubic babes that appeared in the *Ladies Home Journal* in 1909. Her illustrated stories are considered to be the first example of a comic strip. The name "Kewpie" is derived from "Cupid," the Roman God of the erotic. The first Kewpies were made from bisque, and are now worth thousands of dollars. A celluloid version was introduced in 1913. This version became hugely popular and an example was included in the 1939 New York World's Fair time capsule. Toy company Effanbee launched the first, hard-plastic Kewpie in 1949.

Original Kewpies have red and gold hearts on their chests.

This is one of the larger Kewpies made, at eighteen inches tall.

45

LITTLE ORPHAN ANNIE AND SANDY

Created by Harold Gray, Annie first appeared in the *Chicago Tribune* syndicate cartoon strip in 1924. The story features Annie, an orphan, who escapes from a Dickensian orphanage, accompanied by her dog Sandy.

The appeal of the story to children inspired toys like these two charming wind-up Marx tin toys from the early 1930s.

Both toys are clearly identified by their nametags: Sandy's around his collar and Annie's around her belt.

LITTLE RED RIDING HOOD

This charming doll, based on a perennial theme, dates from the 1930s. It is a Vogue "Toddles" doll made of composite material. Because this series of dolls is the precursor to the Vogue signature doll range, the "Ginny," it is sometimes referred to as "pre-Ginny," "compo Ginny," or "#1 Ginny." The Toddles range predominantly featured "little girl" subjects. They were themed dolls based on nursery rhyme or fairy tale characters (as in this case). Alternatively, they were named for their outfits such as "Ice Skater" or "Southern Belle." The dolls' facial features are painted direct onto their composition heads. This can lead to damage, like that to the left eye on this example. Most eyes tend to look to the right. The dolls also have molded-effect hair under their mohair wigs. In time, these wigs can become matted from the combing attempts of young hairstylists, but the wig on our doll is remarkably intact. She is eight inches tall.

A cute glance before the Big Bad Wolf arrives on the scene.

PAPER DOLLS

Paper doll Sandy is shown here with a selection of her outfits. This set was printed in America, and dates from the World War II years. It is a two-dimensional representation of a doll printed on paper, which comes with a set of paper clothing. These dolls were popular due to their cheapness. They were often printed in magazines or catalogs, to be cut out. They were particularly popular during the war years when a shortage of materials led to a dearth of more sophisticated toys.

For all its simplicity, the paper doll was no less effective at entertaining and stimulating young girls, as Ruth Handler, the creator of Barbie, observed in her own daughter.

Costume historians use the paper doll as a prime source of information.

Costumes range from the demure to the daring.

PINOCCHIO

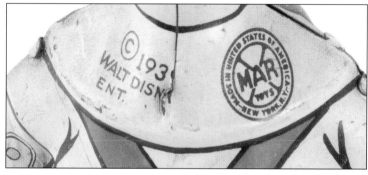

A close-up of the Marx "crossing" logo, which appeared on all their toys, together with the all-important Disney Enterprises copyright, dated 1939.

This charming tin toy is one of a number of toys based on the characters in Walt Disney's series of "Animated Features." These movies were first shown in 1937. *Snow White* was the first of these, and was released by RKO Radio Pictures. This was followed by *Pinocchio* in 1940. Both movies were in Technicolor. The Marx Company, who licensed the characters from Disney, made this toy. It is a windup toy and will walk while its eyes flutter up and down. The printed-on graphics are faithful to the original cartoon illustration.

POPEYE

Popeye with parrot cages is an earlier tin toy made by Chein. It is a windup toy with rollers on the cages, which enable him to walk forward.

Popeye is a grizzled, one-eyed sailor who gets into difficult situations and turns to his can of spinach for strength. This is conveniently located down his shirt. He then knocks the opposition (normally his archenemy Bluto) into next week. Originally appearing in the King Features comic strip *Thimble Theater* in 1929. Elzie Crisler Segar's creation was morphed into a cartoon character by Max Fleischer.

By 1938, Popeye had replaced Mickey Mouse as American kids' favorite character. By 1942, Popeye was enlisted into the U.S. Navy to help with the war effort. The sight of Popeye's pipe spinning in his mouth like a propeller (after a dose of spinach, of course), enabling him to take off like a fighter plane in pursuit of Japanese battleships, is certainly a wonder to behold. His popularity led to a number of Popeye-inspired toys, including this Cameo doll with rubber arms and a cloth body.

PORKY PIG AND PLUTO

Warner Brothers' answer to Disney was the *Looney Tunes* and *Merry Melodies* cartoons featuring Porky Pig, who ended each short with the words "Th-Th-Th-That's all, folks!" The lovable, stuttering pig began his career as a slightly different character in a short cartoon of 1935 entitled *I Haven't Got a Hat*, directed by Friz Freleng. His animator at Warner Bros. was Bob Clampett, who produced his own version of Porky: slimmer, cuter, and with less of a stutter. This is the character on which this Marx tin toy is based.

Our other toy is Mickey Mouse's faithful hound Pluto. Also by Marx, it dates from 1939. The toy has "watch me roll over" printed on his body, and he does just that. The windup motor powers his tail, which flips him over.

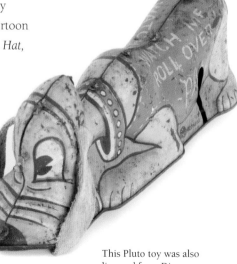

This Pluto toy was also licensed from Disney.

51

RAGGEDY ANN DOLL

Raggedy Ann's charm is her old world simplicity.

This Raggedy Ann doll is dressed in her traditional outfit of striped leggings. She also has several original accessories, including some Raggedy Ann storybooks and a printed plate. Based on a traditional country rag doll, Ann was brought to life in 1915 by John Barton Gruelle, a political cartoonist, to amuse his daughter Marcella. Gruelle illustrated a series of stories featuring Raggedy Ann, published from 1918 onwards. The stories were hugely popular and Gruelle invented a companion for Ann, Raggedy Andy, in the 1920s. Together, Ann and Andy enjoyed adventures in the Deep Deep Woods. Members of the Gruelle family made the first multiple production of the Ann doll in 1918, working in a loft in Norwalk, Connecticut. These first dolls had candy hearts and were sold mainly to promote the stories published by P. F. Volland. Raggedy Ann dolls, like this one, are still available, marketed by Hasbro, and her stories are still in print, published by Simon & Schuster.

WOODY

The simple country charm of Woody wins through against more sophisticated toys in 1995's *Toy Story*. Woody is a 1950s-style cowboy doll suitably attired in a check shirt, black and white cowhide waistcoat, blue jeans belt and holster, a ten-gallon hat, Sheriff's star, boots, and spurs. His head, with its molded brown hair, is made of soft plastic as are his hat, belt, and boots. Press his middle shirt button and he emits a series of witty western epithets such as "Wanna go to a roundup?" "Howdy, partner, my name is Woody," "Yee-haa, cowboy," "Glad to see you, deputy," and so on.

The batteries that power the toy are amazing. Woody's voice is still loud and clear after more than 10 years.

53

AMF JUNIOR ROADMASTER BICYCLE

The American Machine and Foundry company made this AMF Junior Roadmaster bicycle in the 1950s.

Roadmaster Industries was the first to use the Roadmaster brand for cycles. Founded in 1925, the company quickly grew to be an established toy and bicycle manufacturer. Changing its name to Junior Toy in 1929, the company continued to make a wide range of metal-framed bicycles and tricycles under the Roadmaster name.

After two decades of consistent growth, the AMF Wheel Goods Division bought Junior Toy in 1951. An early 1950s brochure for the company described the bicycles as "safely engineered" play vehicles. What more could a kid want?

This bike has been repainted at some time and the training wheels aren't original.

COLUMBIA BOY'S TRICYCLE

The tricycle is still in working order after nearly 120 years.

This Columbia child's tricycle, a model designed for boys, dates from the 1890s but still has most of its original paint. It was made by the Pope Manufacturing Company, which is now known as Columbia. The business began by making and importing bicycles, and was located at 45 High Street, Boston, Massachusetts. Since its foundation by Colonel Albert Pope in 1877, the company has been credited with many firsts in bicycle production, and many consider it to be the founding father of the American bicycle industry. Pope's first self-manufactured cycle was the sixty-inch "Hi Wheeler" that sold for the very considerable sum of $125 when it was introduced in 1878.

55

HAWTHORNE BICYCLE

This gray and blue Hawthorne bicycle dates from the 1940s. It was designed for girls by H. P. Snyder and Company. It has a twenty-six-inch frame and Springer forks. Harley Davidson adopted this design for its motorcycles as an early form of shock absorber for the front wheel. It is equipped with wide handlebars, a full chain guard, and a rear tire guard. There was also a boy's model with fewer comforts.

The tires are period whitewalls, the saddle is sprung for extra comfort, and there is a useful bag platform over the rear wheel. In addition to the Hawthorne, H. P. Snyder was also famous for its Rollfast range of bicycles.

This neat light is from the 1940s.

56

J.C. HIGGINS COLOR-FLOW BICYCLE

Murray Ohio Manufacturing Company made this J. C. Higgins boy's bicycle in 1950. J. C. Higgins was Sears's bicycle brand. Before the Second World War, the company was known as Elgin. Sears retailed this upscale model for $59.99, a not inconsiderable sum in the early 1950s.

The Color-Flow bicycle reflected contemporary auto industry styling of the time, with its chroming and Buick-style "Ventiports" on the side of the faux gas tank. The two-tone gold and red paintwork and whitewall tires echo automotive liveries of the period.

The Color-Flow script on the chain guard has a distinctly 1950s look.

ORANGE KRATE SCHWINN BICYCLE

Long saddles were the biz in the '60s and '70s.

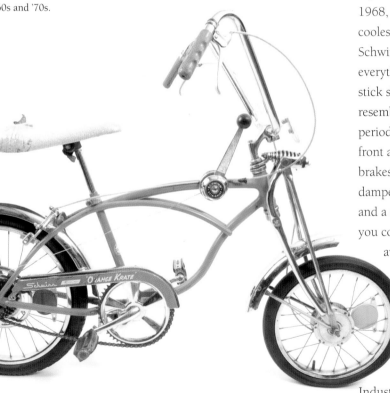

If you had had one of these in 1968, you would have been the coolest kid on the block! The Schwinn "Orange Krate" had everything and more—a chrome stick shift for five gears, somewhat resembling a car quick shift of the period, "ape hanger" handlebars, front and rear cable-operated brakes, Springer front forks, dampers on the rear pillion saddle, and a cool orange paint job that you could see coming from a mile away. Schwinn is one of America's oldest bike manufacturers. It was founded in 1895, and remained a family-owned concern until 1993. It has been part of Dorel Industries since 2004.

STRAWBERRY SHORTCAKE BIKE

Hedstrom made this Strawberry Shortcake bicycle in the early 1980s. Its sweet decals in red, white, and pink make it a model unmistakably designed for girls. It has a sixteen-inch frame, molded plastic wheels, and training wheels. The banana-shaped seat was originally covered in strawberry-printed plastic. The cycle has a fully encased chain and a useful front basket. Muriel Fahrion first drew the Strawberry Shortcake character, whose trademarked graphics appear on the bike, in 1977. She invented the character during her time as a greetings card illustrator for American Greetings's Juvenile and Humorous card department. Fahrion subsequently designed thirty-two Strawberry Shortcake characters for the company's licensing division.

Strawberry Shortcake was totally reliant on this coaster brake for stopping!

59

VICTORIAN GIRL'S TRICYCLE

The design of this tricycle belongs to a bygone era of horse-drawn carts, when cycling became a symbol of emancipation for girls and young women. It certainly gave them a new independence. Dating from the 1880s, it has very little in the way of tires and was known at the time as a boneshaker. The sprung seat resembles that of a pony cart and steering is by a tiller. Power was by treadle-style cranks connected directly to the back "axle."

The design allowed girls to wear conventional clothing of the period, rather than the "rational" cycle wear adopted by many cyclists.

ARCADE McCORMICK DEERING THRASHER

This McCormick Deering Thrasher was made by Arcade in the 1920s. It is made from cast iron and is painted gray with red trim and cream wheels. It comes complete with its original delivery chute. It is nine and a half inches long and has retained most of its original equipment, including the tow bar (which was always unpainted). However, it is missing a bright metal tray at the front of the machine that helps to load the

McCormick Deering is one of the most familiar brands on which farm toys are based.

thrasher, together with the round black and yellow Arcade sticker that was fixed to the rear panel of the model.

Farm toys have been on the market since the 1920s. But since the 1970s they have become the focus of many serious toy collections. This has ensured that these models have become increasingly valuable. Adults and children alike enjoy the hobby, with modelers often displaying their toys in miniature farm scenes that they have created. Nostalgia is almost invariably the reason for collecting farm toys; many collectors grew up on farms.

ARCADE and AUBURN TRACTORS

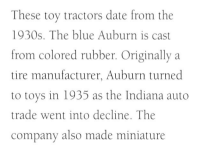

These toy tractors date from the 1930s. The blue Auburn is cast from colored rubber. Originally a tire manufacturer, Auburn turned to toys in 1935 as the Indiana auto trade went into decline. The company also made miniature rubber soldiers that were based on European and American servicemen, such as the Marines and English Palace Guards. Other Auburn farm toys included rubber farm buildings and farm animals.

The two red-painted, cast-iron tractors were made by Arcade and they were based on the popular row crop model tractors of the time. Compared to later die-cast toys these are quite crudely made, lacking the detail of even the Auburn rubber molding.

62

ERTL FARM TURBO 1066

Ertl made this toy International Harvester Farmall tractor with its detailed red body and white-painted metal canopy. The model was originally supplied in a blue cardboard box that proclaimed, "Real wide front wheel movement," "Real deep tread rubber tires," and "Real steering action." These were all accurate claims. The International Harvester Company was formed in 1902, resulting from the merger of McCormick and Deering. The company's original tractors were big, powerful models with names like "Titan" and "Mogul." But then came the first Farmall, a light general purpose tractor, in 1924. By the 1930s, Farmall had cornered sixty percent of the market.

The front suspension has joints to allow the wheels to swivel as it provides "real steering action."

ERTL INTERNATIONAL HARVESTER COMBINE 915

The 915 was the pinnacle of self-propelled, combine harvesters.

This fine Ertl toy is more like a scale model. It faithfully reproduces all the major features of the real thing, with working blades on the eight-row corn head.

In real life, the 915 was a big step forward, with a 150-horsepower engine, a 146-bushel grain bin, a fully air-conditioned cab, power-assisted controls, and an electronic digital monitoring system.

The toy is beautifully finished in classic International colors: red and white.

ERTL INTERNATIONAL ROW CROP TRACTOR No. 415

This die-cast Ertl International row crop tractor No. 415 has fixed steering, but the front axle and all four wheels turn freely. It is constructed in the popular 1:16 scale, and measures around five inches long, two and a half inches wide, and three and three quarter inches high.

Decals with the "International" logo appear on both sides, and the rear wheels have deep-tread rubber tires. The real No. 415 demonstrates one of International Harvester's important contributions to tractor design: its wheels are mounted in a triangular arrangement.

The No. 415 is painted International Harvester Red and has International decals and a printed grill.

ERTL JOHN DEERE 4010 TRACTOR

Ertl made this John Deere 4010 die-cast replica tractor in the 1960s. The success of the company's toys had resulted in a move to larger production facilities in Dyersville, Iowa, and it is likely that this model was made there. The Victor Comptometer Corporation acquired Ertl in 1967, although Fred Ertl, Sr. retained his influence in the company. Ertl preserved its strong position in die-cast toys and

The die-casting process crisply details the engine parts.

replicas, their dominance confirmed by their acquisition of Structo Stamped Steel in 1974. Replicas of

John Deere models have always been successful for the company.

ERTL JOHN DEERE 5020 TRACTOR

The John Deere 5020 model was a development of the 4020 and was first launched in the 1960s. The familiar green and yellow color scheme of John Deere makes the brand a number one seller when it comes to all types of toy farm equipment. Models like this one are highly collectible. This is an original toy from 1966, but Ertl relaunched a 1:16 scale model of the tractor to celebrate the toy's fortieth birthday in 2006. This

original model has fairly good paintwork and the decals are still in position.

A rod connected to the steering wheel operates the linkage on either side of the front wheels to give fully functional steering.

67

ERTL JOHN DEERE B WITH COMBINE

This model is an all-original John Deere Model B tractor with combine, made by Ertl in the popular 1:16 scale. Ertl is one of America's most famous toy manufacturers, best known for its die-cast metal alloy collectibles of farm machinery and agricultural vehicles. Fred Ertl, Sr. founded the company in 1945 and worked there until his retirement in 1992. Ertl was originally located in Dyersville, Iowa, also home to the National Farm Toy Museum.

The combine is extremely realistic; the blades actually turn, driven by a chain from the wheels.

HUBLEY STEAMROLLER

This wonderfully-detailed, army-green Hubley steamroller has a Huber logo on the side. Edward Huber is credited with a long line of agricultural equipment, beginning with his famous mechanical hay rake. The company operated from Marion, Ohio. This fine model is based on steamrollers produced by Huber from about 1910 onward. The green version shown here is quite scarce; the model also came in red. It is an operational road roller with ornate nickel-plating on the wheels and driver and a rotating crank wheel with chain-driven steering. The extremely accurate and crisp castings make this a stunning vehicle. It is seven and a half inches long and dates from around 1935.

Although made from cast iron, the Hubley has plenty of fine detail including chains that steer the front roller—just like the real thing.

LANZ BULLDOG TRACTOR

This printed tin toy is based on the Lanz Bulldog 4016. It was made by Kovap Nachod of the Czech Republic under license from John Deere. The tractor is clockwork. It has a shifting gearbox with neutral, reverse, and three forward gears.

Heinrich Lanz established his machine factory in Mannheim, Germany in 1859. He initially built engines and threshers, but soon started to make tractors. The legendary Bulldog range was introduced in 1921 and Lanz continued to make them until 1956, when John Deere bought the company.

SLIK-TOY TRACTOR

The slogan on the outer packaging of the tractor says, "Ideal for the sandbox farmer" and proudly proclaims, "Slik-Toys a great choice" and "Made in the USA" (something that would be a rare claim today).

The Lansing, Iowa–based company Armor Industries made Slik-Toys from 1938 to 1972. During World War II their toys were wooden—mainly cars, trucks, and tractors all made from scrap wood. When the war ended and metal became available again, production switched to die-cast aluminum because it was lighter and stronger. It was also possible to achieve much greater detail in the finished toys. This cool tractor and plow are from the 1960s.

71

WOODHAVEN TRACTORS

The red tractor has a two-dimensional driver in a yellow shirt and hat.

The Woodhaven Metal Stamping Company of Brooklyn, New York, made these printed tin toy tractors in the 1920s and 1930s. They made a variety of tin toys, including a wind-up bubble blower, a Chinese checkers game, and the St. Louis robot bus, which is a wind-up toy equipped with a belt-driven wheel system. The green tractor shown is a Fordson Model F made in the 1920s. It has far more detail printed onto the tinplate than does the red one: examples are the engine and ribbed gas tank. The tractor has a standing driver clutching a steering wheel.

Viewed from the other side,
the lithographed detail of the
engine on the later green tractor
is subtly different. The red one
is the same on both sides.

This tractor is
powered by
clockwork; the
gears drive the
rear wheels.

BUDDY L FIRE TRUCK

The brass fire bell

Like all Buddy L toys, the front suspension is sturdy, built like a real automobile.

The prince of fire trucks, this 1930s country fire truck has been painstakingly, professionally restored to the highest standards. Made by Fred A. Lundahl's original Moline, Illinois-based company, it has reproduction Buddy L decals in gold, a brass fire bell, and chromed one-piece steel wheels and ladders. The pressed-steel body has been repainted in the correct red enamel, the same as the original finish of the toy. The ladders are mounted on a swivelling turntable in keeping with Buddy L's reputation for being just like the real thing.

CAST IRON PUMPER

Kenton, Arcade, Dent, and A. C. Williams all made versions of this style of fire pumper. Heavy steam pumpers like this were introduced in the middle of the nineteenth century. They were originally hand-drawn, later horse-drawn. Later, they were motorized, like this model. Fire toys of this kind were among the first metal toys and have always had a unique sense of drama for kids in all eras. This one is probably from the 1900s, when cast iron was still a popular material for toys.

The driver has a fire service-style kepi and clutches a steering wheel suspended in midair over the engine cowling.

DENT HOOK AND LADDER

The firefighters are wearing highly-recognizable fire helmets.

The Dent Hardware Company of Fullerton, Pennsylvania made this cast-iron hook and ladder. A pair of horses draws a wagon that has two firemen aboard, in front and back. Firefighting departments started using horse-drawn rigs of this kind in the 1870s, when professional firefighters replaced the volunteers of earlier times. The horses had a wheel beneath them to allow the toy to be pulled along. Dent manufactured many cast iron toys including money banks, automobiles, trolley cars, and locomotives.

DOEPKE FIRE TRUCK

This fire truck comes from the Charles William Doepke Company Inc., located in Rossmoyne, Ohio. Their first toys were launched in 1946. Charles Doepke managed the manufacturing side of the business while his brother, Fred, handled the company's sales.

Doepke prided itself on giving its toys "moving" features. In this case, the ladders swivel on the turntable and elevate by means of a winch. They were made out of heavy grade steel, designed to last, and were retailed for around $12 in the 1950s.

This plastic knurled nut raises the ladder deck and is one of Doepke's moving features.

77

FIRE DEPT. NO. 7

This great, tinplate fire engine, an old style motorized pumper, was actually made in Japan. It is battery-operated with an on/off switch on the side of the truck. It is an excellent example of a high quality *buriki* (Japanese tinplate toy). The Japanese learned the techniques of printing on tinplate from German toy manufacturers who exported their goods to the USA from the mid-nineteenth century onwards. The devastation of the German toy industry after WWI left the market open to the Japanese and their products became available across the country.

The toy is finished in fine-printed detail and colored in gold, red, black, and blue.

MACK-STYLE TURNER FIRE TRUCK

This fire truck dates from the 1920s. It is equipped with two ladders and originally had working headlights, but the bulbs have long been lost. Turner had a range of quality toys built from heavy gauge automotive steel, finished in bright colors. Rubber tires were a standard addition. Turner also used a patented gear motor to drive their trucks. America's first trucks were roughly built using obsolete car parts. John Mack launched the first Mack commercial motor vehicle in 1900, and by 1911, he had a thriving range of purpose-built vehicles including the fire engine on which our toy is based.

MARX FIRE CHIEF

Made by Marx in the 1930s, the Siren Fire Chief is a well-detailed toy with bumpers, grill, grooved running boards, wheels, and hubcaps, as well as details of the outline of the doors. The roof frame is incorporated in the panel stamping. This is a better quality Marx toy than many of the earlier tinplate types, where all body detail is printed on the tinplate. Signs of quality are the battery-powered headlights and a siren driven by the windup motor. The toy is made in sheet steel and is fifteen inches long.

The body graphics that read "1st Batt. Siren Fire Chief" are in very good condition.

STURDITOY FIRE TRUCK

This rare model is the Water Pumper No. 9, from Sturdy. The Sturdy Corporation was founded in 1929 and had their sales office in Providence, Rhode Island. Their manufacturing plant was in Pawtucket, Rhode Island. Two partners established the company: Victor C. Wetzel and Charles I. Bigney. The company made fifteen different models in larger sizes that children would find appealing. These included an American railroad truck, an ambulance, and several dump trucks, made between 1929 and 1933, when the company folded. The toys were direct competitors of Buddy L and Keystone but were made of lighter-gauge steel. This means that fewer toys have survived, thus enhancing the value of those that have.

The Pumper No. 9 has a second rear steering platform that steers the rear wheels.

TURNER RINGING BELL FIRE TRUCK

The fire truck is well equipped with two ladders, a turning winch, and a ringing bell.

The Turner Company of Wapakoneta, Ohio made this truck around 1937. The company was known for the high quality of its toys and this fire truck shows evidence of robust materials that have kept it in good shape. Turner toys were both realistic-looking and colorfully-painted, but despite their quality were offered at competitive prices of around $4.00. This was an advantage during the difficult economic times of the Depression, when toys were a luxury that many American families could not afford.

LOUISVILLE SLUGGER

For more than a century, the Louisville Slugger has been the bat that millions of little ballplayers swing the first time they ever step up to the plate. To this day, baby's first slugger is priced at only $5.00. The origins of the makers, Hillerich & Bradsby, stretch back to the mid-nineteenth century, when German immigrant J. Frederick Hillerich set up a woodturning shop in Louisville, Kentucky. The shop was soon making every kind of domestic woodwork—from balusters to bedposts. Hillerich's son Andrew (or "Bud"), who had been born in the USA, was an amateur baseball player as well as an apprentice in the business. Bud used his father's equipment to turn up his own bats. He started making bats for professional players of the day, including a white ash bat for "The Old Gladiator," Pete Browning, in 1884. (Browning played for the Eclipse, the Louisville professional team.) Gradually, baseball bats became the company's main product. The rest, as they say, is history.

83

OUR GANG GAME

As a young man, Herman Fisher worked for the Alderman-Fairchild Company of Rochester, New York. The company manufactured paper boxes and board games. When a separate company, All Fair Toys, was set up to market their products, Fisher became vice president and held the position for four years. He made an unsuccessful attempt to buy the company in 1930, after which he left to co-found Fisher-Price. The 1930 "Our Gang Tipple Topple Game" was one of

more than a hundred games invented and marketed by All Fair. It was based on a famous series of short comedy movies that featured a gang from a poor neighborhood.

The first of the 220 *Our Gang* movie shorts was released in the silent era of 1922, and MGM launched the final movie in the series *Dancing Romeo* in 1944.

POSTCARD PROJECTOR

The Radio Junior is a type of early 1900s electric projector used to project postcards onto a wall or screen for all to view. This one actually works (although the room must be in full darkness). The front lens and the internal lens are both mounted in a metal tube that slides in and out of the unit to focus the image. It has two postcard-mounting plates so the operator can switch the first card as others view the second. The two chimneys on the top allow the heat from the two electric bulbs to escape. The earlier models used two gas jets that had to be lit from the back. The H. C. White Company of North Bennington, Vermont built this projector.

H. C. White also made an adult version of the Junior, the "Radioptican."

FISHER-PRICE CLOCK

The Fisher-Price teaching clock dates from about 1968 and will be familiar to many baby boomers with younger siblings. It is made from tinplate with printed graphics and plastic fittings, such as the handle and the clock hands. Fisher-Price graphics are always reassuring to young children; the jolly schoolteacher welcomes the cheerful-looking pupils, the friendly spotted dog, the snoozing moon, the waking sun, and the mom shopping in the supermarket. (The only note of discord is the kid who is late for school.) Three partners founded the East Aurora, New York–based company in 1930: Herman Fisher, Irving Price, and Helen Schelle. The founders presented sixteen brand-new toys at the 1931 New York Toy Fair and launched their first product, "Dr. Doodle," as a result. Over the years, the company launched many educational toys; in the 1970s, the company's best-selling line was based on *Sesame Street* characters. Fisher-Price is still running and is a wholly-owned subsidiary of Mattel.

GENERAL STORE

This charming play-store dates from the 1930s. Measuring twelve inches by twenty inches, it comes complete with an awning and miniature packets of grocery products on its metal shelves. It was just one of several large-scale, lithographed tin toys produced by the Wolverine Toy Company. These included dollhouses, the "Number 40"

racing game, a shooting gallery, and a Shell gas station. Wolverine was founded in Pittsburgh,

Pennsylvania in 1903. They continued to make toys until 1950 when the company finally folded.

KOKOMO STOVE

This red and cream Kokomo girl's stove is a live electrical appliance. One way of dating the stove is by the style of its electric cord and plug. In this case, it has been dated to the early 1930s. Many toy stoves of this vintage heated up just like Mom's! Charles T. Byrne and James F. Ryan founded the Kingston Products Corporation in the 1890s in Kokomo, Indiana. (They used the name of the town as a brand name.) Kingston first produced castings for the plumbing industry but soon diversified into toys such as fire engines, racers, and trucks. Some of these were also powered electrically, including one known as the "Fastest Electric Toy Made." The company canceled many of its electric toys when the Depression began.

STOVE AND TEA SET

This cool, pink-enamel stove and washbasin dates from the early 1950s. The stove and washbasin combination is unusual, but the color is not; several toy manufacturers, including Little Lady and Wolverine, made kitchen appliances in pink enamel. This Little Lady stove is electric, and the oven and burners heat up. The whole unit is very lifelike with a faucet, a soap rack, and a fume extractor. The aluminum tea service also dates from the 1950s: three cups and saucers and a teapot, all ready for a doll's tea party!

Miniature collectibles like these are appealing to adults as well as children.

TOY IRONS

These toy irons were made from the 1920s (when cast-iron flatirons were still in use) to the 1930s (when electric irons were becoming popular) through to the 1960s (when irons became a little more streamlined). The classic red and chrome iron is a Wolverine toy, part of the "Sunny Suzy" miniature kitchenware range. This iron has an electrical cord and actually heats up. It was designed as a teaching toy to help girls learn their domestic duties at a time when gender stereotypes were very rigid.

These three types of iron show the development of the iron as a domestic tool.

TOY PHONES

Toy telephones have been around almost as long as the telephone itself, and have reflected its ever-changing styles. This very important toy helps to promote speech and vocabulary, as kids make up conversations with the fictitious person on the other end of the line. The candlestick model has the telephone number "Kiddie 5432." It was made in the 1930s, while the vintage-style payphone dates from the 1940s. Many of America's toy manufacturers—including Remco, Tootsietoy, Fisher-Price, Ideal, Mattel, and Chatty Baby—have produced toy phones

This is a pretty cool copy of an early candlestick phone.

91

TOY REFRIGERATORS

These two toy refrigerators are examples of the girl's toys popular in the 1940s and 1950s. The Snow White refrigerator on the left uses copyright images from Walt Disney's famous cartoon. Its single door, complete with a Snow White monogram, opens to reveal a shelf and two compartments, a fridge and a frost-free freezer. The other, more complex fridge is made by Wolverine and is part of the "Sunny Suzy" range of home and kitchen toys designed to turn young girls into domestic goddesses.

The Wolverine fridge (right) has more detailed graphics, such as on/off switches, ice cube dispensers, and a frozen food compartment.

WICKER DOLL CARRIAGE

This beautiful doll carriage is brilliantly preserved. It is of the kind that you would have seen on many country porches during the early years of the twentieth century. They were traditionally made from wicker—in this case, willow switches. The carriage also has a silk headlining, a turned mahogany pushing handle, and spoked wheels with nickel-plated hubcaps. It is very well built. The carriage is almost substantial enough to carry a real baby. It is possible that Heywood Brothers of Gardner, Massachusetts—a company that specialized in wicker products—made this carriage. Sears Roebuck and Marshall Field also sold wicker baby and doll carriages through mail-order catalogs.

Wicker is an excellent material as it is both light and durable.

93

MASON BANK

This iconic money bank is imprinted with the words "Mason Bank." Made by Shepard Hardware, it dates from around 1887. Most money banks of the time—including this one—were made of cast iron. This one shows two workmen building a chimney. One has a brick hod and the other holds a cement trowel. Like all of Shepard's money bank designs, this one contains an element of humorous activity. In this case, when you put the coin in the hod and press a lever on the right side, the hod carrier leans forward and deposits the coin in the brick wall as the man with the trowel simultaneously raises his arms.

Shepard produced a series of mechanical banks between 1882 and 1892.

94

SAFE

This beautifully-detailed, miniature money safe has a coin slot in its roof. It also has an opening safe door with its own tumbler-style lock. This tinplate toy measures five inches high and is stamped with the word "foreign" on the base, which probably indicates Far Eastern manufacture—possibly Hong Kong. In the years after World War II, many cheap toy imports flooded in across the country from Hong Kong and Japan. The name Orca may be a reference to the classic whale, which was large, powerful, and gray, just as every safe should be!

The fittings on the toy safe accurately represent those of the real thing.

STEVENS TAMMANY BANK

The J. & E. Stevens Company of Cromwell, Connecticut made this mechanical money bank around 1875. Tammany Hall was the headquarters of a Democratic party political machine that used violence and widespread bribery to achieve its political goals; the name "Tammany" has undoubtedly been picked as a satire on greedy bankers seizing your hard-earned money and stashing it in their vault. In this case, you put a coin in the banker's hand and the weight of it causes his arm to drop and deposit your coin in the bank, nodding his head as he does so. The original brown pants help to date it as an early version. Later versions had gray pants.

The toy is made in cast iron and is five inches tall.

TRICK DOG BANK

The "trick dog" is a very popular design for coin-operated mechanical money banks made around the turn of the nineteenth century. At the press of a lever, the dog jumps through the clown's hoop and deposits the coin in the barrel. Several cast-iron novelty specialists, like Shepard and J.& E. Stevens, made these banks, but this example with a solid base was made by the Hubley Manufacturing Company in Lancaster, Pennsylvania and dates from the late 1890s. The words "Trick Dog" are cast into the base, arranged in a semi-circle at the clown's feet. The Shepard version can be identified by its hollow base and the words embossed on the front of the base.

The base of the Hubley version of the toy is a solid, cast-iron casting.

97

AMERICAN RIDE-ON TRAIN

The American National Company of Toledo, Ohio made this maroon and black ride-on train. The company, which was established in the early 1900s by the three Diemer brothers, had the company slogan "Raise the Kids on Wheels." This referred to their range of ride-on toys, which included scooters, pedal bicycles, and sidewalk toys such as trucks and trains just like this one. The sheet steel model is both lifelike and robust. The rivets on the boiler and tender are not real but are stamped into the steel sheet to give a realistic appearance. The child sat on the cab roof and steered the train's front wheels by way of the yellow disc disguised as a steam valve on the top of the boiler.

American National competed with other manufacturers like Keystone, Buddy L, and Marx in the ride-on market.

CHAMPION WAGON

This Champion Wagon dates from the mid-1930s. It has a sturdy pull handle, yellow spoked wheels, a red hauling deck, and the word "Champion" stenciled along each side in yellow. Toy wagons like this are an American classic. Apart from being play objects, many of these wagons helped kids to do hauling and delivery chores on the farm.

The first wagons—originally made of wood—were introduced in the 1880s and remained popular well into the 1950s. The Champion Hardware Company of Geneva, Ohio originally specialized in cast-iron transportation toys as well as making components for other toy companies. Their heyday was between 1930 and 1936.

This wagon is constructed from robust, pressed steel.

FIRE TRUCK PEDAL CAR

AMF made this hook-and-ladder pedal car, unit number 508. One of AMF's main competitors in the pedal car field was Murray, who also made a fire truck. AMF made several versions of their fire truck pedal car, including the "503 Fire Chief," "505 Fire Fighter," "Jet Sweep," "Tote All," and "519 Fire Truck." This was one of AMF's final pedal car models and was very popular. Many have survived. Pedal cars were comparatively expensive and only kids from well-off homes could afford them. Other kids played with things made out of planks and old stroller wheels.

The truck is nicely appointed with a chrome fire bell that actually rings and two plastic ladders.

FORD PEDAL CAR

This Garton-made Ford pedal car was first offered in 1937. Strongly influenced by the Ford styling of the time, the car has bumpers, hubcaps, an aerodynamic windshield, and a hood ornament. It is finished in signature "Garton Red," a color known throughout the toy industry. The Garton toy company, headquartered in Sheboygan, Wisconsin and originally founded in 1878, started out by making wagons, sleds, and wheeled toys. Its first toy catalog was issued in 1887. The company became so successful that it made literally millions of toys; at one time, the factory was the largest juvenile vehicle plant in the world.

The pedal car's paintwork is original and the original decals are still in place.

101

KEYSTONE RIDE-ON FIRE TRUCK

This Keystone ride-on fire truck would have been a highly desirable toy for a young child in the 1920s. Made by the Keystone Manufacturing Company of Boston, Massachusetts, the truck is part of the "Ride-'Em" series. It faithfully includes many features of the real fire trucks of the period. This sturdy, pressed-steel toy is steered via a wooden handle connected to a shaft, which turns the truck's front axle. The child would sit on the metal seat at the rear. The truck is missing some parts, such as the hose and ladders, but the cab-mounted siren and

Other features include steel wheels with rubber tires, headlights, and a cab-mounted emergency light. The headlights still have their bulbs but the cab spotlight bulb has long gone!

radiator-mounted bell are still present and in working order. The

hose reel has a crank handle that still works.

KEYSTONE "RIDE-'EM" STEAMROLLER

This Keystone toy comes from the company's popular line of "Ride-'Em" ride-on toys first introduced in the 1920s. A robust, pressed-steel toy, the steamroller was made at Keystone's Boston plant. Engineered like the real thing, the graphics on the label read "Oil Axles Frequently." All good advice for the young engineer! Keystone made several versions of its ride-on steamroller that varied in length between twenty and twenty-three inches. This is the 1920s model, which measures twenty inches. The rider sits on the corrugated roof of the toy and steers via the wooden handle mounted on the front of the chimney.

The steamroller is equipped with this ringing bell to warn people of its approach.

103

KEYSTONE RIDE-ON TRAIN

A "K" for Keystone logo appears on the wheel hubs and smoke box door.

The Keystone Company's ride-on toys helped it survive the grim years of the Depression. Although they made fewer toys during the 1930s, Keystone remained solvent. People seemed to value Keystone's high-quality, competitively-priced models. This beautifully engineered ride-on train dates from the 1930s and has a cowcatcher, a ringing bell, rubber-tired wheels, and a brake lever. A child could stow his possessions in the tender situated to the rear of the specially-constructed seat. Steering was by the red handle on the top of the boiler. The smoke box door is also detachable, as in the real thing.

KEYSTONE "RIDE-'EM" TRACTOR

The tractor's light red paintwork has survived very well, as has the company logo.

This "Ride-'Em" tractor is from Keystone's successful series of ride-on toys, which date from the 1930s. The "Ride-'Em" line includes a steamroller, a mail plane, a fire truck, a commercial truck, and a steam engine. The tractor has a steering handle, which is mounted on the front, and a pair of large wheels with painted yellow hubcaps at the rear. It has a pair of small wheels at the front; all four wheels have rubber tires. Between 1925 and 1957 the Keystone Manufacturing Company was located in Boston, Massachusetts. The company first made doll wigs, ragdolls, jack-in-the-boxes, and doll voice boxes. Motion pictures helped launch their first toy line in 1919, when Keystone made a moving picture machine featuring Tom Mix and Charlie Chaplin. The company then diversified into making automobile toys and manufactured toy trucks under license from Packard.

The rugged sheet steel construction has withstood years of heavy play.

105

MUSTANG PEDAL CAR

This AMF pedal car was launched in 1965 following the Mustang's 1964 release. This ride-on model is thirty-nine inches long, sixteen inches wide, and eighteen inches high. The model reflects a good deal of skilled workmanship. The pedals are adjustable so that any child of between two and five years old could use the toy. The car was offered in blue and red and had solid rubber tires.

Original toys like this one are highly collectible but new versions made with the original AMF tooling are now available.

106

RADIO FLYER WAGON

Sixteen-year-old Antonio Pasin emigrated from Italy with his parents in 1917. Arriving in Chicago, he struggled to find work even though he was a skilled cabinetmaker. He ended up working for a sewer-digging crew but never lost sight of his American dream.

He invested in some used woodworking equipment, making wagons by night and then selling them by day. Pasin's first wagons were named Liberty Coasters, in honor of the statue that had welcomed his family to their new country. The business grew

and by 1923 he had several employees. Pasin, inspired by the mass-production techniques of the automotive industry, made a new metal wagon from pressed steel. He called this the "Radio Flyer" in honor of two great products of the 1930s: Marconi's radio and the airplane.

Baby boomers loved the Radio Flyer, by then a classic American toy.

ROCKING HORSE

The rocking horse is a perennial favorite. It was first carved out of wood in the eighteenth century, but by the 1940s the traditional horse was overtaken by this pressed-steel version. This Mobo horse was made in England in the late 1940s, manufactured by D. Sebel and Company of Erith, in Kent, England.

The horse was cleverly suspended on a metal frame and "rocked" by four heavy steel springs. The saddle fitment was made of plastic. The brand name "Mobo" was a contraction of the words "Mobile Toys." These toys were also very popular in the States.

Production of the elegant Mobo rocking horse ceased in 1972.

108

BUDDY L OIL TANKER

This Buddy L oil tanker was built between 1925 and 1930. At this time, the company was still known as Moline Pressed Steel; the company acquired its new name in 1930. The truck dates from an era when this premium manufacturer made some of its most collectible and highly desirable toys. Their 1925 model range of twenty toy vehicles included fire engines, moving vans, tanker trucks, lumber trucks, overhead cranes, and sand loaders.

The tanker has its original decals identifying it as part of the Buddy L Tank Line on its faded but totally original red paintwork. The radiator grill was made as a separate stamping and has some traces of its original nickel plate.

As these two views of the truck show, the working headlamps still have bulbs. This is rare.

109

BUDDY L PULL TRUCK WITH DURYEA'S BOX

Buddy L manufactured this pull truck in the 1930s. During the toy's early history, it was customized by the addition of a wooden box. Along the side of the box is stenciled the words: "Duryea's Satin Gloss Starch Manufacturing by the National Starch Manufacturing. Glen Cove, Long Island. Since 1906." Some collectors would say that the box makes the toy non-original but that is how it was played with. In our opinion, the combination of the truck and

The improvised box allowed the toy to be used as a cart.

box make this nineteen-inch tow-along toy unique and highly collectible. The National Starch Manufacturing Company was a real-life concern, which started business on Long Island in the late 1800s.

110

BUDDY L TRUCK

This charming, little blue truck is equipped with working headlights and metal spoked wheels fitted with rubber tires. The truck dates from the early 1930s and is probably from the company's "Junior" model range. Founder

Fred Lundhal's first-ever toy was a miniature truck, which he based on an International Harvester model. Constructed in 1921, it was made from eighteen- and twenty-gauge steel that he recycled from his company's scrap metal pile. By

1925, his range of toys had expanded to twenty items. As the decade wore on, he added more features and greater realism to his models. He introduced the "Junior" line of trucks in 1930.

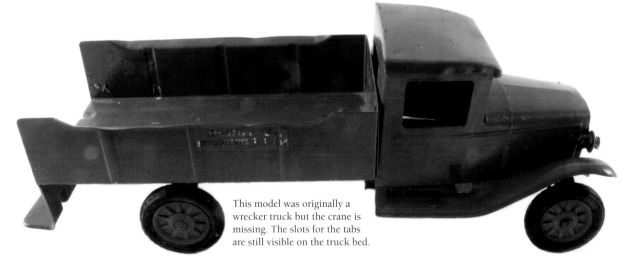

This model was originally a wrecker truck but the crane is missing. The slots for the tabs are still visible on the truck bed.

111

CIRCUS ON WHEELS

Harkening back to the heyday of touring circuses, this charming Wild Animal Circus truck was made by Buddy L in the 1950s. Although the circus theme was unusual for Buddy L, it wasn't a complete anomaly. They also produced a truck-mounted carousel on wheels. Their standard range was more down-to-earth: farm trucks, fire trucks, and road haulage trucks. This model stayed on the company's product listing for several years. A later, white-painted version had the same three doors, marked "Tony," "Leo," and "Jumbo."

Rival manufacturer Kenton brought out their "Overland Circus Bear Wagon" to compete with Buddy L's circus on wheels.

DUMP TRUCK

Buddy L made wooden trucks during World War II but returned to more conventional materials after the war. By that time, like many other toy manufacturers, they were using more plastic in their toy lines. However, it is pressed-steel toys like this classic 1950s style dump truck that appeal to collectors and toy lovers the world over. This example is unrestored, but it is possible to buy new transfers and decals, fenders, and headlights to replace Buddy L parts that are worn or missing.

By the 1950s these wheels and tires were made of plastic.

113

FARM SUPPLIES TRUCK

Dump trucks have been an important model in the range of all major toy manufacturers since the 1920s. The large-scale, pressed-steel truck, pioneered by makers like Buddy L. Steelcraft, and Keystone, made a lot of sense: kids could haul materials in the back. The dump truck became a signature model for the company and as auto-styling evolved, so did the styling of the toys.

This particular truck has its original yellow and blue paint scheme and the Farm Supplies decal is still in good shape, even though it dates from the early 1940s. It has a mechanical

dump action with a linkage that opens the tailgate as the bed is raised, and a metal prop at the front to support the tailgate once it is up. The toy is twenty-three inches long.

The rugged construction and mechanical simplicity of this toy have ensured that it has lasted well.

KEYSTONE STEAMROLLER

This charming steamroller is made of heavy-gauge sheet steel with pressed-metal fittings. These include the roller, steering and pulley wheels, the bell, and the stovepipe chimney.

Manufactured by the Keystone company of Boston, Massachusetts in the 1930s, it was designated Model No. 60. The model's general construction and solid wheels convey the power and weight of the original. The

The Keystone Steamroller is twenty-six inches long.

corrugated cab roof of this ride-on toy is very strongly built to bear the weight of a young driver.

115

KEYSTONE TRUCK WITH SACKS

This green and tan pressed-steel dump truck was made by Keystone and measures twenty-six inches in length. It has a C-cab and manual dump, and is a valuable and highly collectible item. At first, Keystone manufactured toy motion picture machines (the Keystone Moviegraph) and produced children's comedy films. Their first venture into manufacturing pressed-steel model vehicles was under license from Packard. They made small versions of the company's production trucks. Fierce competition with their main competitor, Buddy L, led Keystone to add many interesting refinements to their toy vehicles. These included nickel-plated hubcaps and radiator caps, engine cranks, transparent celluloid windshields, working headlamps, and rubber tires. After World War II, most of Keystone's toy manufacturing output was based on tools and dies that the company had acquired from the defunct toy division of Kingsbury.

The nicely constructed scale farm sacks must have been bought separately by the customer as they are not part of the original toy.

MACK STEAM SHOVEL TRUCK

Chein Hercules made this early Mack Steam shovel truck. It is now a very rare toy indeed. This style of vehicle, which would have been obsolete even by the 1930s, was probably made between 1910 and 1920. The lithographed graphics on its wheels read, "35 x 6 Made in the USA." Lithography was one of founder Julius Chein's specialties. It was an idea he borrowed when a friend who worked at the American Can Company told him how his company's cans were lithographed rather than painted. This early Mack Truck is pretty basic: it has no windows and the wheels are solid.

The toy has a crank handle and a winding mechanism that raises and lowers the fully-functional shovel.

This robust truck has survived in perfect working order but its paint finish has suffered.

MARX LAZY DAY FARMS TRUCK

The Lumar division of Louis Marx and Company manufactured this vintage tin truck. It is around five inches high and seventeen inches long. Both the cab and the trailer are heavily lithographed with various details including headlights

This superb graphic of a farm scene is an example of how good the Marx lithography process was.

on the cab, wooden slats on the trailer, and the "Lazy Day Farms Registered Stock" poster. This form of lithographed tin plate is inexpensive to produce and demonstrates the Marx company ethos of providing good toys at competitive prices. "Give the customer more toy for their money" and "quality is not negotiable" were the maxims on which Louis Marx had founded his business. The company became increasingly successful, and by 1921, they had taken over the manufacture of their own toys.

METALCRAFT HEINZ DELIVERY TRUCK

This cool Heinz delivery truck dates from 1932. Metalcraft of St. Louis, Missouri licensed its graphics from Heinz. Its original decals mention several of the Heinz company's famous 57 varieties including Rice Flakes, Spaghetti, and Tomato Ketchup.

This comes from a range of toy trucks that were endorsed by famous brands and was known as the "Business Leaders" series.

The decals celebrate Heinz as a famous American brand.

This early truck has die-cast wheels and rubber tires with "Goodrich & Co" embossed on them.

119

NYLINT MOBILE HOME

The detachable trailer has glazed windows and a working door.

This Nylint mobile home probably dates from 1964. The truck pulls a dual-wheel trailer and the whole assembly is around thirty inches in length. The piece has charming decals including the "Mobile Home" decal on the trailer and the "#6600 Nylint Mobile Home" decal on the truck. The model was produced during a crossover period in Nylint's well-documented history that fell between its "Ford Motor Company Era" and its "Mod Styling Era." In this latter phase, Nylint (originally Ny-Lint) removed the Ford logos from its pressed-steel vehicles, but they remained heavily influenced by generic Ford styling.

Like with this mobile home toy, Nylint tended to give its models several action features, which greatly enhanced their play value.

NYLINT TRUCK AND TRAILER

The truck and trailer are finished in a cool, 1960s light blue.

This light blue and white Nylint truck and trailer set was made in the early 1960s. It comes from

Nylint's Econoline range of toys, which were based on real Ford models of the same name. Although these toy trucks were remarkably similar to the real thing, many people actually preferred Nylint's styling to Ford's. Econoline was an extremely popular line of toy

vehicles produced between 1962 and 1972. Early models had Ford decals, but later ones are branded "Nylint," as can be seen here.

The range included several variants including an identical truck without the stake bed, plus a fully covered model.

121

TONKA SAND LOADER

Mound Metalcraft got started in 1946. After an early foray into garden tools the company decided that toys were the way to go. By 1947 they were presenting their iconic range of sturdy, pressed-steel trucks at the New York Toy Fair.

Right from the start, the company's emphasis was on strongly-built construction toys that really worked. Two of their first offerings were the No. 100 steam shovel and the No. 150 crane.

This excellent sand loader and truck comes from the 1950s. It has a stepped, rubber belt that can be cranked up to raise sand from the hopper onto the bed of the dump truck. The truck itself has a side-positioned lever that raises the flatbed into the tipping position.

The Tonka Sand loader logo is applied to the truck as a transfer.

This robust lever lifts the truck flatbed.

TOYLAND FARM AND TRANSFER WAGONS

Among the many vehicles Marx made was the Merchants Transfer wagon, complete with the Marx "NYS" crossing logo. This ten-inch toy is drawn by a team of two horses and equipped with solid metal wheels. Next to it is Marx Toyland dairy truck, which (complete with its balloon tires) measures around fifteen by nine inches. This single-horse-drawn, lithographed toy van is a wind-up model decorated with a delightfully rustic "Toyland's Farm Products" graphic. The models date from the 1920s and 1930s.

TURNER TRUCK WITH BOWLING PINS

This Turner truck was manufactured at the company's Wapakoneta, Ohio plant in the early 1930s. It has rubber tires fitted to red-painted metal wheels, running boards, and an open cab with a rotatable, pressed-steel steering wheel, which is connected to the front wheels. It has a fixed friction flywheel similar to the hill climber mechanism still popular for powering toys in the 1930s. In the back of the truck is a collection of wooden bowling pins and balls. These are not original but are part of the toy's heritage as this was how its young owner played with it. The toy is fifteen and a half inches long.

Despite its worn condition, this early Turner dump truck is highly collectible.

VINTAGE STEAM SHOVEL

Prestigious maker Buddy L manufactured this vintage steam shovel sometime between 1921 and 1931. Constructed from heavy gauge metal, it has stood the test of time very well, although the paint has mostly worn away. More than just a toy, this is an accurate depiction of a true steam shovel with its lifelike boiler and coal boxes. The articulated arm of the shovel is raised and lowered by a handle-turned winch. The roof is sturdily constructed from corrugated steel.

The back view of the steam shovel shows the boiler firebox door.

125

BENJAMIN PUMP GUN

The slogan of the St. Louis and Benjamin Air Rifle Company was "The Gun That Shoots."

Before about 1925, air guns were just for kids in America. But with the advent of weapons, like the Benjamin, which were not only powerful but also relatively silent, adults started to take an interest in them as well. This example, which dates from 1937 to 1938, is a Model .300 (BB caliber). It is very similar in appearance to the later Model .310. The .300 has a bronzed steel barrel, although earlier versions were made of brass with a walnut stock. The pellet is fired along the upper tube, which is, in effect, the barrel. It is mounted on top of the cylindrical air reservoir that runs virtually the entire length of the gun to the rear of the trigger. The Benjamin was considered one of the best airguns available in the 1930s, since it was not only very powerful but also properly engineered out of the finest materials, just like a real gun.

BUFFALO BILL RIFLE

The Daisy and Heddon companies combined for a while to produce this magnificent BB gun. It dates from the late 1960s and has the words "Buffalo Bill Scout" engraved on the side of the polished-steel action. The twin over-and-under barrels follow the classic Winchester pattern and there is a carbine sling ring at the front of the fore-end. As with all Daisy BBs, the gun is cocked by pulling down the ring at the back of the trigger guard. The stock is made from wood-effect plastic and has an engraved medallion inset in the right side. This celebrates "Buffalo Bill Chief of Scouts." The model designation of the gun is 3030. It most closely resembles the Model 1866 Winchester "Yellow Boy" carbine. This gun was made at the traditional home of Daisy guns in Rogers, Arkansas.

BUZZ BARTON SPECIAL

Way back in 1932, Daisy made history when they were one of the first manufacturers to name one of their guns for a personality. Buzz Barton was a circus performer who became a Hollywood actor during the silent screen era. Born William Andrew Lamoreaux in Gallatin, Missouri in 1913, he was known by a number of aliases before becoming "Buzz Barton: Boy Wonder of Westerns." He endorsed the original Daisy Model 195 as the Buzz Barton Special, which had a walnut stock, blued metal, and a working scope sight. The first models had a paper label on the left cheek of the stock. Subsequent models, starting with the 103, had the logo branded into the stock in a star-shaped (later an oval-shaped) Buzz Barton motif. Stocks were made in both light maple and dark mahogany. The example shown here is a later model. Early models are now rare and increasingly valuable. Poor old Buzz, like so many of his contemporaries, didn't make the transition into talkies.

CAPS AND AMMUNITION

The real thrill of playing cowboys and Indians was hearing the satisfying crack of the cap exploding, the puff of smoke from the breech, and the enticing aroma of cordite.

The trouble was that not every cap detonated, and the blue rolls with bigger blobs of explosive performed much better than the cheaper red rolls with hardly any charge.

Manufacturers were in tune with their young customers and strove to make their products more reliable and realistic. The "Shootin' Shell" range by Mattel was particularly good, and the "Greenie Stik M Cap" (see the center of the display) was stuck on the end of the shell case like a real primer.

129

CAST-IRON PISTOLS

These are some of the oldest examples of toy guns, dating back to the very beginning of the twentieth century. The Dixie pistol at the top dates from the 1920s, but the company made toy pistols as early as 1894. The middle gun is a Federal-Kilgore, made by the Federal-Buster Corporation of Homestead in Pittsburgh, Pennsylvania before World War I. The models in the range were marked "No.1," "No. 2," and so forth. This is a No.1, making it the oldest gun on the page!

The bottom gun is a Kilgore, manufactured in the 1930s when the company was operating out of

Dixie pistol

Federal-Kilgore pistol

Kilgore pistol

Westerville, Ohio. It is marked "Made in the USA" and has the original patent date of December 1914. All of these guns have a real quality despite their lack of detail. They have the weight of real guns because they are made of cast iron. This makes them more realistic than the later, pressed tintypes.

CAST-IRON CAP PISTOLS

Kilgore cap pistol

Hubley Flash cap pistol

1937 Dandy Hubley cap pistol

With the advent of the silent Western, guns regularly appeared on the screen, creating a demand for more realistic-looking toy guns. Kilgore made the gun at the top left of the page. It is closely based on the 1935 Colt Trooper and dates from the late 1930s. This was a cap gun that one loaded by hinging the barrel and chamber forward. The hexagonal nut shows a repair to the pivot. The top right gun is a Hubley "Flash" from around 1934. The cylinder on this model actually revolves—a significant advance in toy design.

The third gun is also a Hubley—on this occasion, a 1937 Dandy Model. It has a revolving cylinder but has evolved into a hinge-out type, controlled by the movable rod at the front of the frame.

131

COLTS

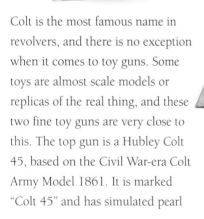

Hubley Colt 45

Nichols "Stallion 45 Mark II"

Colt is the most famous name in revolvers, and there is no exception when it comes to toy guns. Some toys are almost scale models or replicas of the real thing, and these two fine toy guns are very close to this. The top gun is a Hubley Colt 45, based on the Civil War-era Colt Army Model 1861. It is marked "Colt 45" and has simulated pearl plastic grips. It also has a working chromed loading lever under the barrel (which is sometimes missing on this toy). The cylinder is picked out in a contrasting gold-colored plating. The gun is a massive fourteen inches long. The lower gun is a Nichols "Stallion 45 Mark II" finished in bright nickel with black monogrammed handgrips marked "N" for Nichols. It is closely based on the Colt .45 1873 Peacemaker. Both guns date from the 1950s and 1960s.

CORK GUNS

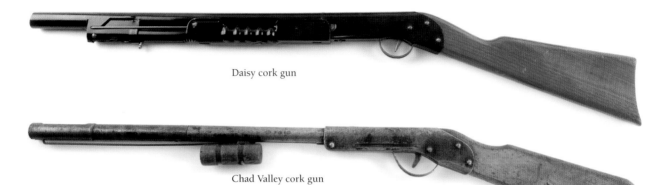

Daisy cork gun

Chad Valley cork gun

Cork guns were a favorite with kids of a bygone age, long before the advent of electronic laser toys.

The upper cork gun for younger children was made by Daisy. It is based on a real-life Remington carbine–style riot shotgun. It has the traditional Daisy feel about it, with a wooden stock, authentic pressed metal barrel, and a black-painted slide action. The spring that fires the cork from the barrel is tensioned by the lever under the barrel and is released by pulling the trigger.

The lower gun is much older. It was made in England in the 1930s by Chad Valley toys of Harborne, Birmingham, a company that was started by Anthony Bunn Johnson in the early 1800s and named for a small stream that shared the valley with the factory. The gun works by compressing air into a chamber at the rear of the barrel, which is pumped up by means of the under barrel slider. The gun is made of pressed steel painted black, with a wooden stock. Its overall length is twenty inches.

133

COWBOY BOOTS

These classic children's boots are based on authentic western footwear. The rope-style boot has more rounded toes and heels, while the more "dude ranch" style has ornate stitching and pointed toes. Westerns became very popular in the 1950s—when shows like *The Lone Ranger* and *The Cisco Kid* were on television—and kids inevitably wanted to dress up like their heroes. Cowboy hats, simulated cowhide waistcoats, and chaps were on sale in most toy stores. Many were cheap interpretations of the real thing, but others were more realistic. These perfectly-scaled-down cowboy boots must have cost a doting parent a small fortune.

The style of these boots dates them to the 1940s.

These boots are plain black cowhide.

DAISY MODEL 1894 AND DAISY DOUBLE BARREL

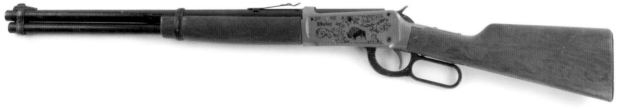

Here are two guns from the Daisy Company, representing totally different ends of their market. The double barrel shotgun is a child's cork gun but is still remarkably well made and detailed. It has two triggers and a carved wooden stock. It dates from between 1955 and 1960.

The other gun is part of the Daisy "Spittin' Image" range, which was introduced in the 1960s. This particular series of toys set out to offer BB guns that were based on iconic, real-life guns, like the Model 1894 Winchester. Here is the Daisy version of the gun, designated the Daisy Model 1894. The gun has a wooden stock, brass-plated side plates with engravings of buffalo hunting scenes, and an adjustable front sight. The Winchester was by far the best-selling toy gun but other models offered were the "Model 26 Remington Fieldmaster" and the "Colt 45 Frontier Revolver."

135

DAISY POWERLINE

"Danger Not a Toy" says the advertising literature for this gun. This is literally true, as even in .177 caliber, the gun has plenty of punch. The Daisy Powerline Model 880 was launched in the 1970s and was Daisy's first pneumatic system gun. The gun was a serious departure from the fun but harmless BB guns of Daisy's past. The new gun could fire either BBs or waisted lead pellets, which were more accurate. The reservoir is charged by pumping the underlever. Broadly speaking: the more pumps, the more power. The upper limit was around 700 foot-pounds, which is pretty good for an inexpensive gun. The original 880 was made of steel and had wooden stock. The latest version of the gun (which has now been on sale for over forty years) is mostly plastic. It retails at around $40.00, which upholds Daisy's consistent value-for-money approach.

DAISY PUMP ACTION

The Daisy Model 25 was the most widely sold air gun ever made. Designed by Fred Le Fever, it was manufactured between 1914 and 1986. In that time, over twenty million guns were produced. The guns were made at the Plymouth, Michigan factory before production moved to Rogers, Arkansas in 1958. The gun was cocked by pumping the slide under the barrel. The fifty-pellet magazine detaches from the barrel for loading. Over the years, production of the gun has changed subtly with the use of different materials. The original versions were all steel and wood, but the gun has now evolved into one with many plastic parts. These two examples exemplify the difference. The top gun is much later. It has a plastic stock and die-cast receiver with faux engraving. This gun is much lighter than the earlier model (below), which has the traditional wooden stock and steel receiver. This is probably the nicer of the two guns.

DAISY RED RYDERS

"Boy, that's a Daisy!" was the reaction of the general manager of the Plymouth Iron Company of Plymouth, Michigan when he fired designer Clarence Hamilton's new spring piston gun. The year was 1886, and the company, which produced farm windmills, was looking to diversify its product base. The gun had been designed to give away as a novelty incentive with the company's windmills. But the toy weapons generated more interest than the windmills. This was an era when gas-powered and electric machinery was on the rise, replacing the older wind-driven technology. The company gradually changed to full-time production of the Daisy guns. The iconic Red Ryder range was introduced in 1938. It was named for the comic strip cowboy, who appeared in numerous movies between 1940 and 1950. Special features of the gun were the saddle ring with its leather thong and the engraved stock. The lower gun is a Model 39, the forerunner of the Red Ryder.

DERRINGER BELT BUCKLE

A new breed of hero emerged in the television shows of the 1950s. Unlike the rugged cowboy heroes of the 1940s who had fistfights, shootouts, and horseback chases, these new characters (like Maverick) were more subtle and refined. They carried concealed weapons in the sleeves of their dandified jackets. Young cowboy fans began demanding toy pocket pistols. This cool "Buckle Gun" by Mattel is one

product inspired by this trend. The die-cast buckle depicting a single-shot derringer and a single shell could be worn on a belt. Push

out your belly and out pops the gun. The buckle has the words "Remington Derringer 1865" embossed on it.

DIE-CAST CAP GUNS

Bronco

Gene Autry model

Bango-O

Several cap gun manufacturers turned away from cast iron in the 1940s and began using die-cast alloy instead, as this material was easier to work with (it is lighter and makes it possible to achieve finer detail in the casting). The gun at the top left of the page is a "Bronco" by Kilgore, which dates from the early 1950s. It has a bucking bronco cast into the frame and a mountain lion on the barrel. The white plastic grips have a saddle and boots molded onto them. The top right gun is a 1940s "Gene Autry" model made by Kenton.

The bottom gun is a 1940 "Bang-O" made by J. & E. Stevens of Cromwell, Connecticut. It fired a roll of 50 caps that was loaded by dropping the barrel and has "Bang-O" cast into the frame and a horse's head on the grips.

FANNER 50 IN BLACK

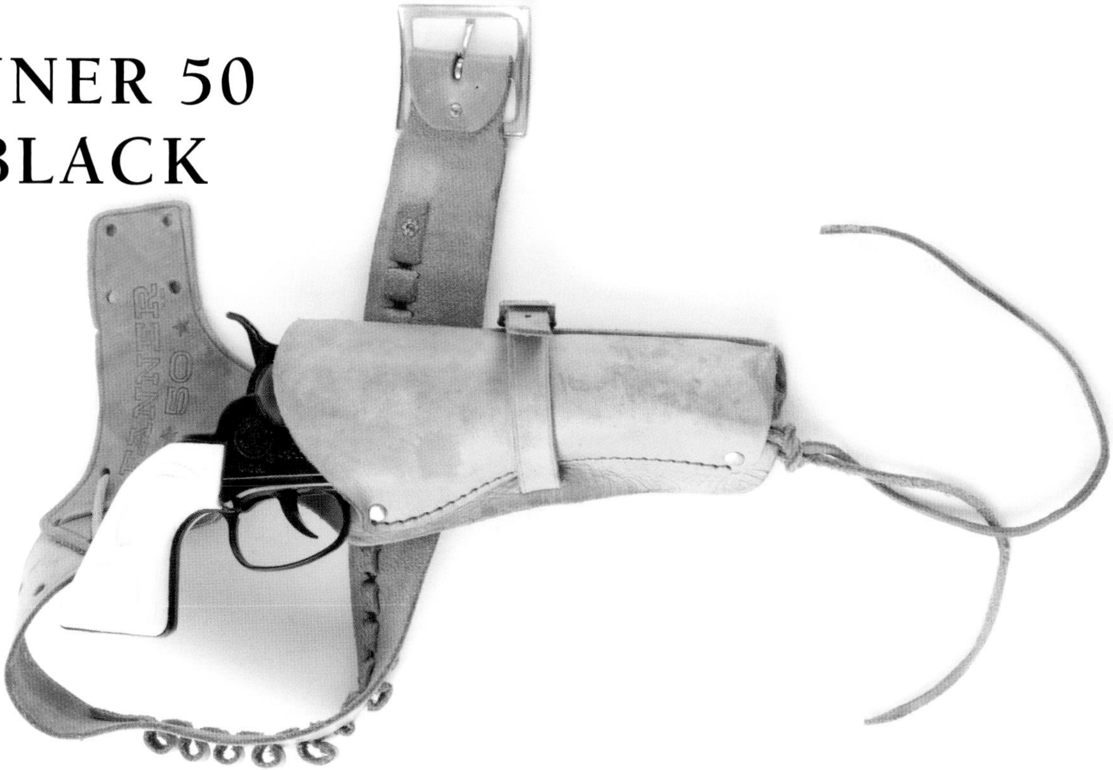

The Fanner 50 was one of Mattel's greatest successes of the early 1960s. This rare gun dates from 1961 and was made to tie in with Chuck Connor's short-lived follow up to *The Rifleman* television series: *The Cowboy in Africa*. It can be identified by the impala head on the grip. The holster shown here is from an ordinary Fanner 50 and the original black holster is missing. The name Fanner describes the firing action; "fanning" the hammer feeds the caps through, firing them as you go.

141

FOUR TOY PISTOLS

To the serious Western fan, these goods were just novelty items.

Back in the 1950s, when realism began to be important, kids wanted to own toy guns from companies like Fanner and found earlier, cheaper tin toys much less interesting. The gun second from the right, by Wyandotte, is a five-star dart gun that had a strong spring inside and shot darts from the barrel. The two on the left are Marx "clicker" pistols: when the trigger was pulled, the guns made a loud clicking noise. The gun at the far right is a lithographed Japanese tin toy from the early 1950s. This is the kind of gun that would be for sale in dime stores. It has "Cowboy" lithographed onto the grips. It fired darts or corks.

FRONTIER SCOUT RIFLES

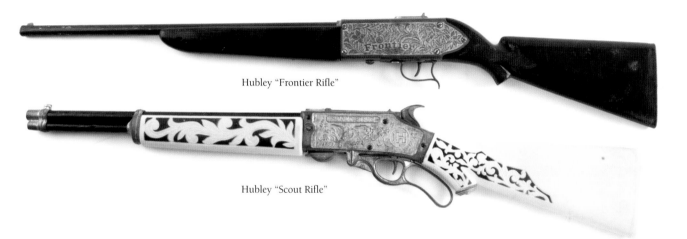

Hubley "Frontier Rifle"

Hubley "Scout Rifle"

These two Hubley toy rifles can be regarded as "his 'n' hers." With its fancy white stock, the "Scout Rifle" (bottom) was specifically marketed to 1950s "cowgirls." It has two short barrels with a band and is based on the Winchester 1866. The lever action pulls down to load the reel caps into a tray. The words "Scout Rifle" are engraved into the side plate. The gun is thirty-three inches long. The boy's model was the "Frontier." It has a single barrel and has "Frontier" engraved on the side plate and "Hubley MFG" cast into the buttplate. This gun does not appear to be based on any particular real-life model. It also has a tray for loading the caps, which drops down from under the mainframe. It is thirty-five inches long.

143

HAHN BB GUN

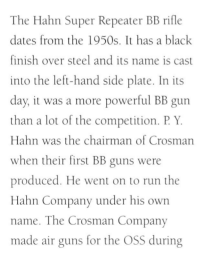

The Hahn Super Repeater BB rifle dates from the 1950s. It has a black finish over steel and its name is cast into the left-hand side plate. In its day, it was a more powerful BB gun than a lot of the competition. P. Y. Hahn was the chairman of Crosman when their first BB guns were produced. He went on to run the Hahn Company under his own name. The Crosman Company made air guns for the OSS during World War II. These were designed for use in special operations where silence and stealth were important. Special agents had to live off the land and an air gun was ideal for this purpose. The war generated demand for increasingly powerful air guns. The Hahn BB gun was also very attractive, with accents of the Winchester Model 1903 to make it appealing to children. It is thirty-four inches long.

HUBLEY DAVY CROCKETT

Davy Crockett was a real-life backwoodsman from Tennessee. In the 1950s, actor Fess Parker turned him into a screen legend. Walt Disney Productions launched the eponymous television show on December 15, 1954 and the movie *King of the Wild Frontier* premiered the following May. "The Ballad of Davy Crockett" (sung by the Sandpipers) and the movie music (by the Mitch Miller Orchestra) both hit the charts, and children went wild for coonskin hats and Davy Crockett muzzleloaders. Hubley already had this classic toy Buffalo Rifle in production. The name is embossed on the patchbox lid on the stock. To cash in on the Davy Crockett craze, Hubley sagely embossed the words "Davy Crockett" onto the fore-end, just in front of the flintlock side plate. This simple marketing move turned an existing gun into an instant bestseller.

A close-up of the die-cast metal flintlock action shows a buffalo-hunting scene engraved on the side plate. Hubley is famous for this level of detail.

HUBLEY TEXANS

Here are three examples of Hubley's die-cast range of Texan cap pistols. They date from the 1950s. The guns were available in different colored, metal-plate finishes: here we have gold, silver, and pewter. Hubley manufactured 11,184,878 toy pistols in 1952, many of which were Texans like these; they were the most popular cap guns around.

As some American states didn't allow guns that fired caps, Hubley also produced some special guns with dummy hammers to get around this legislation. The top gun is an example of this. All three have the Hubley signature plastic handgrips with steer heads molded into them.

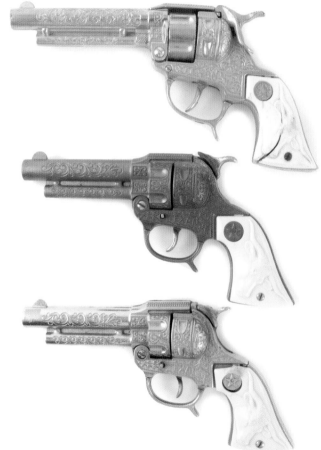

HUBLEY WESTERNS

The Hubley Manufacturing Company of Lancaster, Pennsylvania was long renowned for its well-made and attractive cast-iron toys. But by 1940, the cost of producing cast-iron toys had become prohibitive, so Hubley (the largest producer of cast-iron toys and cap pistols in the world) began to change production to die-cast zinc alloy toys. This "western" line was a very popular range of die-cast guns. Although they have been described as "rather simple guns," they are perhaps only simple by Hubley's own high standard of accuracy.

The range was done in nickel plating, which has mostly worn off these two examples. The brand "Western" is cast in the frame, just

above the trigger. The handgrips came in a choice of colors. Here they are blue and white, but brown and green were also available. A steer's head is molded into the plastic grip, while a cast star motif held the grip at the top. On this model, the barrel broke downwards to give access to the cap compartment. The guns were repeaters and took roll caps,

just like the box of Star Brand caps shown. The gun is eight and a half inches long.

147

KENTON CAP PISTOLS

Up to the 1920s, early cap pistols were crudely made toys. They had names like "Oh Boy" and "Big Bill" and had no particular Western connection. They were stylized approximations of guns rather than toy versions of real weapons. When moviegoers began to see realistic guns in the silent films of the 1920s, they demanded more authentic toys.

Early cap guns were called "revolvers" but had no "revolving" moving parts. They were cast in two halves, and were held together with steel pins. Their big, clumsy hammers fired round, single-shot caps. Kenton made the top two guns, while the bottom gun is by Stevens.

The Kentons have a "K" cast into their handgrips, while the Stevens has an "S."

148

LONG TOMS

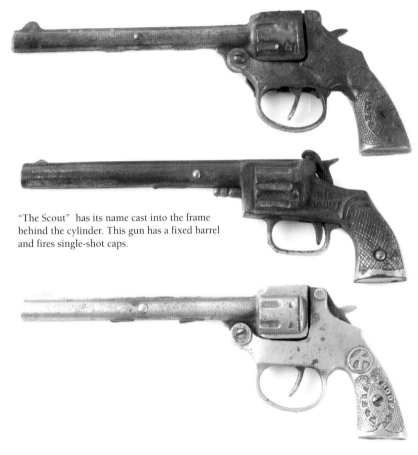

"The Scout" has its name cast into the frame behind the cylinder. This gun has a fixed barrel and fires single-shot caps.

Kenton made these distinctive, long-barreled pistols. By the 1920s, cap guns had become a major line for the Kenton Lock Manufacturing Company of Ohio. These toy revolvers were known as Long Toms because of their unusually long barrels. They actually look like the cowboy guns used in the silent movies. The top and bottom guns are the same model, but one is in a better state of preservation than the other. They date from 1928 and have the words "Trooper Safety" cast into the handgrips, together with a "K" for Kenton. The barrels break down to load the caps. The middle gun is a model from Stevens called "The Scout." Its name is cast into the frame behind the cylinder.

149

MAVERICK PISTOL

A late 1950s advertisement for the *Maverick* television series starring James Garner.

When ABC launched their original comedy-western series back in 1957 with James Garner in the starring role, they created a new genre in western entertainment. Nobody could ever quite take Bret Maverick seriously, until he reached for his gun, and showed himself to be unexpectedly good with it. This merchandised gunslinger-style pistol and holster, copied from the one used on the show, was made by Esquire Novelty/Leslie-Henry. It is a bronze, long-hammer, revolving cylinder pistol, with white stag grips and a very fancy leather holster.

NICHOLS DERRINGERS

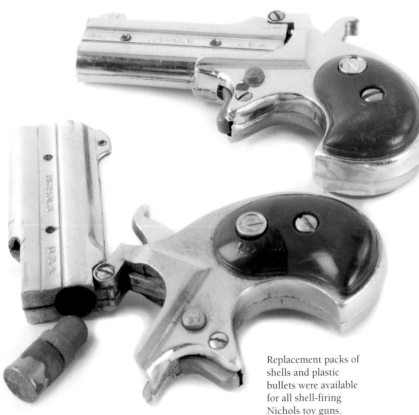

Replacement packs of
shells and plastic
bullets were available
for all shell-firing
Nichols toy guns.

Two brothers, Talley and Lewis
Nichols, founded Nichols
Industries in Pasadena, Texas in
1945. The company
concentrated on cap guns of
all sorts. Its guns were
extremely realistic, like the
two Derringers shown here.
They have high-quality nickel
finish and wood-effect handgrips.
The guns break just like the
Remington single-shot Derringer
that they so strongly resemble. A
three-piece bullet comprised of a
case, shell, and red plastic pellet is
primed with a Stallion round cap.
This fits into the breech, and when
the trigger is pulled, the pellet is
fired.

151

PALADIN HOLSTER

Paladin's business card with the motto "Have Gun Will Travel" nestles between his twin revolvers.

"Have Gun Will Travel" was the motto of Paladin, the gentleman-scholar turned gunslinger. Craggy-faced Richard Boone starred as the man in black clothes, who righted wrongs for a fee of $1000. This handsome holster and belt in black leather is decorated with pressed-metal, white knight chess pieces on each holster, tie-downs, and a silver buckle. The belt has "Paladin" printed on it and has loops for fourteen spare bullets. Leslie-Henry of Wilkes-Barre, Pennsylvania made the guns for Halco Distributors (originally the J. Helpern Company of Pittsburgh, Pennsylvania).

152

PAPER SHOOTERS

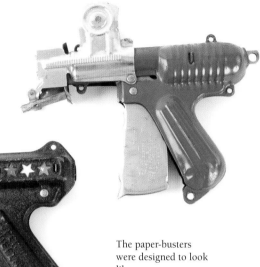

Described by the manufacturer as "absolutely harmless," these three "paper-buster" guns date from 1940. They originally sold for twenty-five cents but are now extremely collectible. The guns were made by the Langson Manufacturing Company of Chicago, who started by making industrial tools, dies, and stampings. Paper-busters produce a loud *bang* without the use of caps. Langston marketed them as a sideline to its core business. The guns used strips of scrap paper that were fed into the top. As the trigger was pulled, the paper was stretched tightly against a rubber grommet, creating a tight seal. Simultaneously, air was compressed in a chamber inside the

The paper-busters were designed to look like space guns.

gun and released. It exploded through the paper and caused a loud bang. The company also produced toy torpedoes and a cannon that worked in the same way.

153

PIRATE GUNS

Hubley "Pirate"

Hubley "Flintlock"

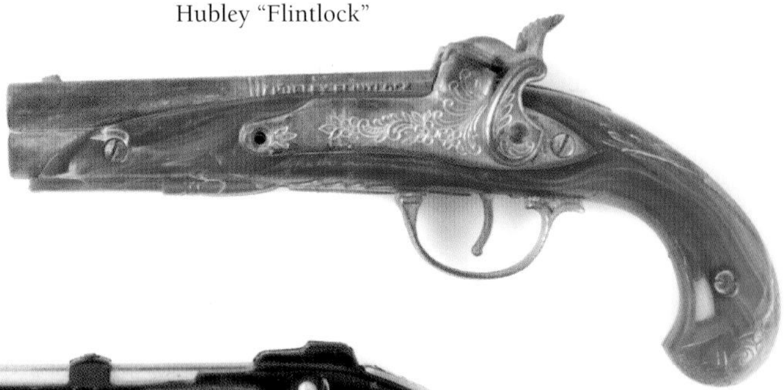

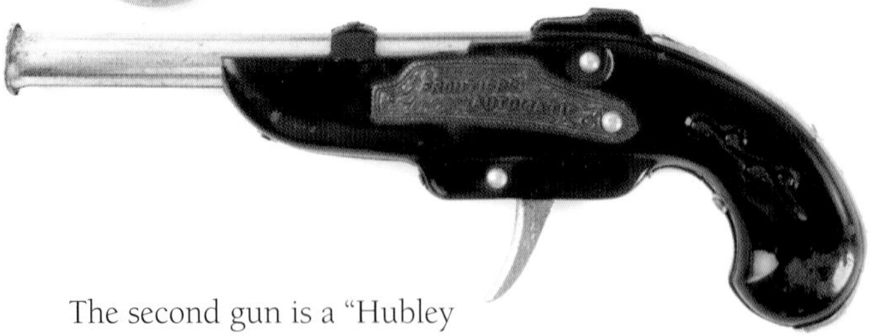

Hubley "Frontier Automatic Cork Pop Gun"

When children weren't playing cowboys and Indians, they often liked to play pirates. The author himself used to dress up with a bandana, a patch over one eye, and an old plaid scarf over one shoulder. A favorite element of buccaneer play was to heft a Hubley "Pirate" like the one shown here. This represented a double-barreled flintlock gun. It was remarkably accurate for the times, with its scrolled trigger guard, barrel engraving, lock, and hammers. It even had its own ramrod.

The second gun is a "Hubley Flintlock," the name cast in heavy capital letters into the barrel; again it is a double-barreled weapon with twin hammers, filigree engraving on the lock and barrels, and a very authentic wood-effect butt. The third gun at the bottom is a "Frontier Automatic Cork Pop Gun"—perhaps a bit more Davy Crockett than Davy Jones!

154

RODEO JOE

The Unique Art logo is printed on Rodeo Joe's gas tank.

The Unique Art Manufacturing Company of Newark, New Jersey made the "Rodeo Joe Crazy Car." It is marked "Made in USA Patent pending." This wind-up tin toy features detailed graphics with western-styling themes like "leather" stitching, ropework lettering, the bucking horse on the front hood, and the longhorn cow on the grill. Everything with a western theme was popular in the 1950s, especially the cowboy outfit. Joe has cowboy boots, striped pants, a checked shirt, a cowhide waistcoat, and a ten-gallon hat in the true western tradition.

155

ROY ROGERS

In the 1950s, "The King of the Cowboys" was featured in movies and a long-running television show. With his smart horse, Trigger, Roy Rogers inspired a generation of young fans who wanted to be like their all-American hero. This fringed suede jacket was styled after one of Roy's own.

SHOOTIN' SHELL FANNER

By the 1960s, realism had become very important and this gun was at the head of the field. The "Shootin' Shell" system was developed by Mattel for their Fanner range. This allowed the owner to put caps into the actual cartridge, and then load the cartridges into the revolving cylinder. They were just like the real thing! The "greenie" caps and spare bullets for the gun are shown on page 129. The gun is high-quality, nickel-plated, die-cast metal fitted with plastic "stag horn" grips. The gun was based closely on the Colt 45 Peacemaker and was produced between 1959 and 1965. It is eleven inches long.

TWIN HOLSTER SET

These two guns are Hubley "Cowboys" and are twelve inches long. They were supplied with this pair of leather holsters, which are punched with Hubley's "H" trademark rivets and pressed-steel wheel motifs. The belt has an embossed shield showing a wagon train scene and a silver-colored, western-style buckle and tip. It is thirty-three inches from tip to tip.

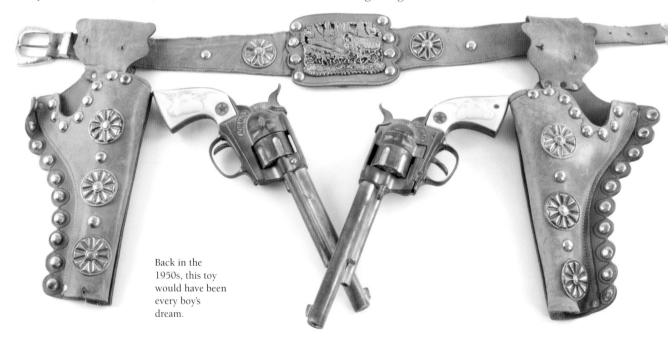

Back in the 1950s, this toy would have been every boy's dream.

WESTERN ACCESSORIES

To the serious juvenile western fan of the 1950s and 1960s, the right accessories were very important. A cool Marshal's badge, a pair of handcuffs hanging from your belt, and a pair of spurs jingling from beneath your chaps were absolute essentials. These accessories didn't cost much. Consequently, many toy manufacturers offered whole ranges of western accessories. The items featured in this collection are all from these decades. The lawman stars are in die-cast metal and plastic. Was Billy the Kid really ever a Sheriff?